ExtraOrdinary

An End of Life Story
Without End

Michele Tamaren
Michael Wittner

PEARLSONG PRESS
NASHVILLE, TN

Pearlsong Press
P.O. Box 58065
Nashville, TN 37205
www.pearlsong.com
www.pearlsongpress.com

Cover painting by Annette Nicolas. Heart drawings by Herman Liss.
Michele Tamaren photo by David Tucker Photography.
Book & cover design by Zelda Pudding.

Trade paperback ISBN: 9781597190619
Ebook ISBN: 9781597190626

Library of Congress Cataloging-in-Publication Data

Tamaren, Michele, 1947–
  ExtraOrdinary : an end of life story without end / Michele Tamaren &
Michael Wittner.
      p. cm.
  ISBN 978-1-59719-061-9 (original trade pbk. : alk. paper)—ISBN 978-1-
59719-062-6 (ebook)
  1. Liss, Herman, 1909–2004. 2. Liss, Herman, 1909–2004—Death
and burial. 3. Jews—United States—Biography. 4. Older Jews—United
States—Biography. 5. Death—Psychological aspects—United States. 6.
Death—Social aspects—United States. I. Wittner, Michael, 1990– II. Title.
E184.37.L57T36 2012
973'.04924—dc23
                                2012005621

Advance Praise for
ExtraOrdinary

"In a world where our Western elders have forfeited
their own wisdom, here is a book that calls them back,
that tells them the road is possible. Even greater,
it denies nothing of their struggle, but uses that
as the way and the giver of blessing."

Megan Don
Award-winning author of
Meditations with Teresa of Avila: A Journey into the Sacred

"A must read!
ExtraOrdinary: An End of Life Story Without End is
at once unique and universal. With brilliance and depth,
Michele Tamaren and Michael Wittner write of love, loss
and the enduring human spirit. This is a book that
enters your heart and touches your soul."

Ellen Frankel
author of *Syd Arthur* & *Beyond Measure*

"*ExtraOrdinary* is a page-turner!
Although I never met Herman Liss, I feel I now know him
and am inspired by his modesty, goodness, and ability
to delight in life, even at its most difficult.
Written with clarity and insight,
this book is itself a delight."

Rabbi Elie Kaplan Spitz
author of
*Does the Soul Survive? A Jewish Journey to Belief in Afterlife,
Past Lives and Living With Purpose,*
& *Healing From Despair: Choosing Wholeness in a Broken World*

IN LOVING MEMORY OF MY HEART-SISTER, HEDY LOPES,
whose laughter and spirit still enliven my own.
MICHELE TAMAREN

TO HERMAN LISS—
an invaluable teacher, mentor, healer, and friend.
MICHAEL WITTNER

THEIR MEMORIES ILLUMINE OUR WORLD

"There are stars whose light reaches the Earth
only after they themselves have disintegrated.
And there are individuals whose memory lights the world
after they have passed from it.
These lights shine in the darkest night
and illumine for us the path...."

HANNAH SENESH
1921-1944

CONTENTS

Dedication 5
Acknowledgements 11
Foreword 14
Preface 17
Introduction (MICHAEL) 19
Introduction (MICHELE) 22

PART I 25
Herman Liss—To Life! 26
Betty Leavitt—A Light 38
The Dance 48
The Wedding 57
Autumn Love 61

PART II 68
A New Life 69
Transitions 75
Devotion 82
Soulmates 88
A New Home 95
Dark Night 102
Welcome Home 112

PART III 116
Meeting Michael 117
Meeting Herman (MICHAEL) 118
The Reign 122
Our Second Visit (MICHAEL) 124
Invitation 126
Our Bar Mitzvah (MICHAEL) 128
The Soul's Journey 130

Born Knowing 137
Card Games (MICHAEL) 140
Friends Who Became Family 142
There Are No Words 145
Four-Legged Love 147
The Hearing Heart 149
Herman & Others 150
Still Growing 152
The Embrace 154
Struggle & Strength 157
Halloween 161
A Mensch & More: The Story of Herman Liss (MICHAEL) 164
A Movie & More 168
The Premiere 173
Life is a Journey 178
A Teacher & a Healer 183
Sunset (MICHAEL) 186
Toward the Light 192
The Bikur Chalem Shul (MICHAEL) 196
Sailboats (MICHAEL) 198
Herman's Heaven 201

Epilogue (MICHAEL) 205
Epilogue (MICHELE) 208

The Twelve Neverending Truths of Herman Liss 215
Michael's Reflections 216
About the Authors 219

ACKNOWLEDGEMENTS

WITH BOUNDLESS LOVE, JOY, AND GRATITUDE I thank all those who helped to inspire, nurture, and birth *ExtraOrdinary*. I shall be forever grateful to Reverend Dr. Ruth Ragovin, who gently guided its shape. Susana Stella Maris and Sally Schrieber-Cohn saw its light when it was still a spark. My Pod 2 Claritas Sisters—Martine Amundson, Laurie Blefeld, Ginger Sudas Buckley, Joan Dresher, Angie Hinkley and Mary Sheehy— blessed our book in its infancy. How grateful I am to Ellie Lite, a woman who could have been my mom's best friend, for reading the manuscript with the eyes of a loving mother.

Thank you, too, to "Herman's Girls," who helped to lift Herman and Betty in manifold ways, and heartfelt appreciation to Chang-Chen Chen for sharing her special wisdom and compassion with my parents. Irish, Italian, Taiwanese, Jewish, Christian, Buddhist—daughters, all.

With profound appreciation I thank the skillful, loving souls whose hands and hearts supported my parents and myself during the darkest times. The names and descriptions of some of the medical personnel, staff, residents, and institutions have been changed to honor confidentiality.

There are authors who have literary agents—I have a Literary Angel. Ellen Frankel, herself a writer, asked if she might share the manuscript with her publisher, Pearlsong Press. With delight I learned that Pearlsong's president and publisher, Peggy Elam, holds the vision of *Healing the World One Book at a Time*. Working with Peggy has been a writer's dream.

Deep gratitude to our most recent readers, Analesa Rose, Devorah Feinbloom-Rosenberg, Mimi Nelson Oliver, Stephen Hicks, Becky Shepard, and Phyllis Karas for their invaluable insights. Also, warm appreciation to Jeff Ferrannini and Marla Gay for their meticulous editorial work. Thank you to Elcenir Carvelho, Dara Fruchter, and David Tucker for their artful contributions. My heartfelt appreciation to Annette Nicolas, whose brilliant light shines through the cover painting.

How grateful I am to my co-author, Michael Wittner, for helping Herman to reclaim his life. What a privilege to watch Mike grow from an empathic and generous youth into a gifted and compassionate young man.

Abundant appreciation to my spiritual teachers, who have nurtured my soul's growth. Special love to my dear family—my husband David, our son Scott and daughter-in-law Cindy, and my brother Barry for your priceless love and encouragement. You are my treasures.

MICHELE TAMAREN
January 2012

ACKNOWLEDGEMENTS

FIRST, OF COURSE, I WOULD LIKE TO THANK HERMAN Liss. I could go on for pages and pages about Herman— and, well, I did. Not many people move you to write an entire book, but Herman was that rare gem. I miss him every day. An emphatic thank you to Michele Tamaren, without whom this book would have never been written. For almost half my life now, Michele has been a beneficent presence, always helping and encouraging me. She has been a surrogate mother and a dear friend. I needed an entire book to write about Herman, and I might need another one to write about Michele. I'm truly indebted to her.

Thank you to my family—it was actually my father's idea to make a movie about Herman, and he helped me film and edit the project. Dad, Mom, Allie, even Jazz—you're my entire life. You know how much I love you and I'm here to say it again.

Thank you to Peggy Elam and Pearlsong Press—thank you so much for this incredible opportunity. You've been a pleasure to work with, and I'm so happy we serendipitously found each other.

Thank you to the staff of the Shalom Center—during Herman's first dark days there, he was crowned King Ahasveros of the Purim story. Throughout his whole stay there, you treated him like a king. You were all so enthusiastic about our project, and helped us every step of the way.

Thank you to all the fascinating people I've met along the way—the aides, the friends, everyone who took an interest in our project. You colored an already colorful experience, and I look forward to meeting many more of you.

MICHAEL WITTNER
January 2012

FOREWORD

Extra*Ordinary: An End of Life Story With-out End* may seem at times like fiction, but I know firsthand that it is very real. Herman and Betty Liss were my friends, although nearly twice my age. We met when I was in my early forties, and our friendship flourished for more than ten years. Herman and Betty taught me many lessons, but the sweetest was this: It is never too late to have a happy childhood and a happy life.

We became more than friends—we were family. You see, I called Betty and Herman my "therapy parents." My own parents, escapees from Nazi Germany and Poland during WWII, had died several years before I met the Lisses. My parents had endured the loss of loved ones in concentration camps, and they were riddled with grief, anxiety, and fear. I was an only child raised in a home shaded by worry and negativity.

As an adult, I now understand and forgive. But then this amazing duo came into my life—Herman and Betty Liss. Their daughter, Michele, introduced us. I had never met anyone like them. Optimistic, forward-thinking, open, sharp and witty, overflowing with unconditional love for their own children, they quickly embraced me and I them. Before long Herman and Betty had gained not only another daughter but several more, because with open hearts they welcomed all of Michele's close friends into the warm and broad extended fold.

Being with Herman felt like being wrapped in a blanket, calm and comforted. With a quiet presence he exuded that feeling of "things will be all right." Herman seemed at peace with himself and the world. I often wondered what it would have been like to grow up with a father like him.

Betty was as gentle and refined as Herman, yet there was another side to her. She could be irreverent, bold, and wickedly funny. Our brand of humor was very similar. We were both keen observers of life and not afraid to tell it like it was. We could be bitingly funny and rather impatient—none of which seemed to bother Herman. He never appeared to mind that Betty, who sometimes seemed bigger than life both in her physical presence and manner, stole center stage. He was proud of her. Also, I believe that Herman felt content with himself and never needed to take the spotlight away from anyone else.

It might be odd for someone my age to develop a deep friendship with people who, at the time, were around seventy-five and eighty-five years old. I say "friendship" because even though they were of my parents' era, strangely enough they were in so many ways like my contemporaries. We ate out, always fighting about paying, and they usually prevailed. Other times we went to shows and concerts or just talked. Once they were seated safely, freed from the confines of their walkers, they were my peers.

No topic of conversation was off limits or inappropriate. Not that *we* were always appropriate. Once, in an upscale Cape Cod restaurant, Michele, Betty, and I were acting just like junior-high schoolgirls, overcome by paroxysms of laughter at who-knows-what silliness, clutching our stomachs and putting our heads under the table trying to regain control. And Herman, always refined, just sat there and gave his sweet smile. He was not embarrassed—he was proud of "his girls" and happy that they were having such a good time.

When Herman's beloved Betty died, we all worried. How would he cope? Would he decline and fall into a depression? Would he eat? Would he ever connect with anyone? After all, given his age of ninety-three, his own physical limitations, the enormity of his loss, he could have been expected to fail very quickly. As you will read in the book, ultimately our fears turned out to be unjustified. Herman was much stronger than we knew. His natural optimism, his curiosity, his lack of fear, his openness to new opportunities, his respect and regard for everyone allowed him, like a rose in late bloom, to continue to flower. The bloom stayed on that rose a long time. Deep down, though, I knew—we all did—that Herman was waging an inner battle between wanting to join his beloved Betty and wanting to cherish and enjoy life.

Herman turned my notions of aging upside down. He defied every stereotype. He did not exhibit frustration, crankiness, anger or self-pity. When seated in his wheelchair, talking or reading, the years would disappear. I rarely thought about his infirmities, nor did he. We were too busy talking.

Herman told many stories about his youth, and also talked proudly about his long career as a food salesman. But by no means did Herman focus solely on the past. He avidly read the daily papers and studied and discussed complicated religious and secular texts. I was astonished by the depth of Herman's thinking—the intellect, insight and the wisdom that emerged. And I was delighted to discover the person who was inside all along.

Michael Wittner, the thirteen-year-old volunteer who became Herman's dear friend, also enlivened Herman's days. The two would talk current events, politics, Red Sox, school—life—never at a loss for conversation despite the generations between them.

We, too, shared eagerly, and 5 p.m.—Herman's dinnertime—came far too quickly. I never was ready to take leave. Nor was I ready to take leave of him on May 7, 2004.

I LOVED HERMAN DEEPLY. How could you not love him? His memory serves as a blessing to me and to everyone who knew him. My wish is that by reading this wonderful book, you come to know Herman and Betty and that you, too, receive such a blessing.

Thank you, Herman, for all that you taught me. And thank you, Michele, for bringing both Herman and Betty Liss into my life.

HEDY S. LOPES
Acton, Massachusetts

PREFACE

"**I**'M JUST AN ORDINARY MAN."
That's how Herman Liss invariably described himself when questioned about his humanity by family and friends and even the press. Herman was humble and largely unaware of his magic—his gift for inspiring hope and wholeness in everyone he met. At the end of his life this man without advanced degrees or riches or robust health was wealthy beyond measure. He shared his abundance through his wisdom and humor, his love and kindness, his patience and compassion. An ordinary man? You decide.

In his nineties, Herman became a healer and a teacher. He journeyed eighteen months from loss and despair to connection and peace. Along this path Herman touched and changed countless lives as his own was coming to completion. From hospital to rehabilitation center to nursing home to hospice, Herman's words and smile elicited love and laughter.

Rather than a tragedy, this is a story of growth and learning, a joining of generations and cultures and hearts.

ExtraOrdinary shares the story of an ordinary man with an ever-evolving spirit. It is above all a love story. It tells of the undying love between a man and a woman, between parent and child, between friends who became family, and between an elderly man and a young boy.

The story is written in two voices. Michele Tamaren is Herman's daughter, not by blood but by blessing. Michael Wittner came into Herman's life as a twelve-year-old student volunteer who became Herman's best friend. Their eighty-year age difference dissolved as

Herman and Michael visited each week in the nursing home. The first draft of *ExtraOrdinary* was completed in 2005 when Michael was just fifteen, his heart and memories young and fresh and tender.

Michael's writing is identified by his name at the top of his chapters. There are scenes in which Michele and Michael reflect on the same encounter, each from their own perspective. The reader has the opportunity to enter into the story both through the eyes of an adult and the heart of a child.

The book unfolds in three sections. The first explores Herman and Betty's early years and adult lives prior to their improbable meeting, their romance and late-in-life marriage. Part Two shares their deepening commitment through Betty's illnesses and passing. The final section invites the reader into an end of life journey that traverses from shadow to light.

SIX MONTHS BEFORE HERMAN'S PASSING, Michael and his father, Ben, began to film the story of his mentor's life. At the premiere of the movie Michael paid tribute to Herman. One of the many journalists present quoted Michael in a feature article. "I see a little of God in Herman every time I'm with him. I think I've become closer to God in knowing this man."

An ordinary man? Well, perhaps. Perhaps each of us has the ability to choose an extraordinary path, a life that shines light into the hearts of others, a life touched by the Divine.

MICHELE TAMAREN
MICHAEL WITTNER
2012

INTRODUCTION
MICHAEL

FIFTY PEOPLE SAT EXPECTANTLY AT THE PREMIERE of our movie, but it felt like a thousand. As our film was projected onto a screen, I knew that the friendship between Herman Liss and me would probably last forever.

There were many little similarities between us. The last two digits of the years we were born needed only to be reversed to be identical—1909 and 1990. When Herman was younger, he physically resembled me. We were both Jewish adults, even though I became one in the midst of my friendship with him at the age of thirteen at the time of my bar mitzvah. He had been one for eighty-one years. We laughed at the same jokes and had similar political views.

The premiere of our movie was on Thursday, April 22, 2004. I felt as though it was a second bar mitzvah. We picked out invitations and wrote a program, and I remember the growing feeling of anticipation as many people walked into the Shalom Center's movie theater.

This was my second big event shared with Herman. But this time it was all about Herman. It was a celebration dedicated to his life, an event few people experience.

I had a speech all prepared—however, I wasn't prepared for the wait. We arrived early precisely because my family always arrives late. This time we came too early. We sat outside the lobby of the movie theater, reading the Shalom Center's *Generations* magazine, waiting for guests to arrive.

"What if everyone forgets to show up?" I asked my dad.

"That won't happen. We're early. Let's go over what you're going to say in front of the press."

It was weird to hear this. I did what many kids had done before—visit the elderly. I had decided to visit Herman once a week, and now all of a sudden I was a low-budget independent "filmmaker" about to be interviewed. The press—I didn't quite know what to say.

"All right. Go ahead."

"So, Michael—look at me, always look at me—" my dad coached—"Why'd you decide to make this film?"

"Well," I said, "I decided to make this film because of Herman. Herman is one of the most remarkable people I've ever met. I came to the Shalom Center every week and I listened to Herman, to his stories, to his lessons, to his beliefs, and though the idea didn't come from me—it came from my father—I knew it was the perfect idea—to record Herman not only as a keepsake for myself, but as a keepsake for everyone, including Herman himself."

The answer may not have come out exactly in this form, but it was what I was thinking. My reply came to evolve over time, from the shaky and disjointed answer to a smoother, more articulate response.

"Good, but always, always maintain eye contact. So, Michael, what were your visits like with Mr. Liss at the Shalom Center?"

"Well," I explained, "when the typical visit began, I'd walk into Herman's room. He'd be facing the window, in contemplation, either reading a book or just sitting. I'd tap him on the shoulder and he'd turn around, and delight would spread across his face. This wasn't just with me, mind you—he gave this greeting to everyone he knew. He'd shake my hand, laugh, and invite me to sit down. We'd discuss anything that was on our minds. The afternoons were ordinary, but I always felt so welcomed, so happy, so light-hearted. Where does the time go, we always wondered, when at the end I'd wheel him to the dining room and he'd tell me to see him next week. That was a typical visit."

"I think you're ready," my dad said. "Just remember what I told you about eye contact, and you're good to go." He returned to reading his book.

Thanks, Dad, I thought as I sank into the strange feeling of just me and my memories.

Down the hall I saw Herman being rolled like royalty to the movie theater. I'd heard the Shalom Center's CEO had lent him a tuxedo, because Herman was such a classy guy.

I didn't expect to see what I saw. I really don't like using schmaltzy metaphors, but all of Herman, especially his face, *was* glowing radiantly. He looked thrilled. He was king for a day—and I was genuinely proud of what I had done for this man.

The auditorium inside the movie theater, quaintly named "Movies at Mom and Dad's," was gradually filling up. Michele had invited many people—nurses, friends, relatives, and residents. Slowly, what we thought would be a small, private showing escalated to over fifty people. Herman greeted each warmly, as if he'd known them his whole life. He was continually pausing and posing for the cameramen and guests who wanted a shot of him.

When the film began the DVD player skipped, and the voices weren't in sync. Fortunately we had a spare VHS tape. As the film began to play in front of a large audience for the first time, I watched the reactions—including Herman's.

Because I had made the film, and started from scratch, and edited it for hours, it never occurred to me that it could have such a powerful impact. Even when I saw the finished product for the first time, I had a hard time being objective because I knew it so well.

Here, as Herman watched the movie dedicated to him unroll on the big screen, his shoulders sagged and he began to weep, especially at the montage about his late wife. I can't fathom how he must have felt, experiencing such a profound mix of emotions all at once.

Once it was over Herman was happy to talk to the newspaper reporters. I was just surprised. I felt very important as one of them took me aside after the movie to "have a word with me."

I saw Herman chatting with reporters. He was giving them information to put in an article, and I realized how lucky they were to have Herman as their subject. In the middle of my interview I looked over at Herman, saw him in the midst of a similar interview, and smiled to myself.

We brought Herman back up to his room after everyone had left. He sat by his bed, laughing and reflecting on the day's events. When it was time for us to go, Herman shook my hand and said, as he always did, "Thank you, Michael, thank you!"

INTRODUCTION
MICHELE

"**S**TEPFATHER." THAT'S WHAT ALL THE NEWSPAPERS called him, but they were wrong. Herman Liss was my father. He may have come into my life when I was grown, but he was the dad of my dreams.

Herman married my mother on August 18, 1974, his sixty-fifth birthday. Betty, my mom, was fifty-five. This was the second wedding for them both. My mother had been married to my biological father for twenty-five crisis-filled years, and Herman's wife had died on their first anniversary. Neither Herman nor Betty expected, nor even desired, to marry again. Neither, I suspect, wished to risk another heartache.

Their meeting, their marriage, their love was magic. It healed and sustained them for an amazing twenty-eight years. Even my mother's death at eighty-three did not break their bond. Herman longed for her—yearned to hold her, to touch her, to dance with her again. That longing pulsed through Herman until his final breath.

One week to the day of Betty's funeral, Herman suffered a serious stroke. He had just lost his beloved, and now his health, his home, his independence. Most tragically, Herman lost his will to live. At ninety-three Herman's spark began to dim—he wished only to die. Yet miracles restored his soul.

Lives intersected, angels appeared, minds expanded, synchronicities unfolded, and light began to flow back into Herman's world. Healing came not only to a remarkable elder but also to those who entered into this sacred circle. Each of us—different ages, races, religions, and cultures—opened to fresh possibilities. Small stirrings gave birth to new life ribboned with rich awareness, appreciation, love, compassion, and joy.

Herman's hearts, drawn in gratitude by Herman for those who shared their own hearts with him, grace this book as an offering to the readers. May your own heart receive and share the universal flow of kindness.

STEP-DAD—NO. For myself and countless others, Herman Liss became the father who taught that when we are open, love and family, wholeness and peace can manifest lifelong.

PART I

HERMAN LISS—TO LIFE!

"**C**ONGRATULATIONS, MRS. LISS. IT'S A BOY!**"** exclaimed the doctor. "Your prayers were answered. Meet your little miracle."

"Thank God! Thank God!" Rose Liss rejoiced as she raised her hands in praise. "Jacob, come, come—we have a son!" Rose called to her husband in Yiddish.

Jacob threw open the bedroom door and dashed to embrace his wife. Together they marveled at their perfect infant, their fourth child, their first boy.

"And what will you name your new little blessing?" asked the doctor.

"Chaim," beamed his father.

"Chaim," echoed his mother.

"Life! That's Hebrew for life," said the doctor in English.

"Herman, we will call him in English. Herman Liss."

"Herman Liss, born August 18, 1909," intoned the doctor as he recorded the newborn's information. "May you, Herman, be blessed with a long, healthy, and happy life. *L'Chaim*—To Life!"

HERMAN WAS BLESSED FROM BIRTH. He was cherished both by his parents and by his three older sisters. The little girls—eight, six, and four—were as excited as Jacob and Rose by this fascinating new addition. Herman became his sisters' baby doll. While their mother cooked and cleaned and sewed, the girls played house and dressed Herman in their own hand-me-downs. They pushed his well-used carriage through the neighborhood and included him in their daily tea parties.

Gentle and loving by nature, Herman learned to respect and adore women, but he was all boy.

Herman grew tall and strong and handsome. He inherited his mother's flashing blue eyes and his father's thick, curly dark hair. His smile melted hearts.

Herman's parents had emigrated from Poland in 1903, fleeing from the pograms in which Jews were targeted, tortured, and killed just for being Jewish. Jacob and Rose, along with their two eldest daughters, settled in New London, Connecticut, joining other family in the coastal town. Jacob, a shoemaker by trade, found work as a cobbler in a rickety little shop. He rose before dawn and returned home after dark, earning a meager wage for his expanding family. The Lisses rented a small cold water flat on the second floor of a drafty wooden two-family home. As Herman got older, he and his father shared a narrow bed in a room off the kitchen, and his mother slept with the girls in the bedroom.

What the family lacked materially, they made up for in laughter and love. Herman's mother was a stately woman whose embrace was as warm and comforting as the fresh baked breads she prepared each Sabbath. Rose's Jewish faith was central in her life, and each Friday night the candles were lit and the blessings recited. She kept a kosher home and taught her four children the commandments. More important, she lived them and lived by the Jewish tenet *Tikkun Olam*, healing the world through charity and lovingkindness. Each week Rose put aside coins for charity and joined with other neighborhood women to provide for others who had even less than they. Rose embroidered tablecloths and towels for orphan brides to create a dowry they would not have otherwise. To save money Rose bought broken crackers for her own family, so she might buy flour to share her homemade Sabbath bread with those who had none.

As Jacob labored and Rose raised the children, she held a dream. One day, when her little ones were grown, Rose intended to go to night school. There she could to learn to read and write in English and study American history and government. Then, like her children, she, too, would become an American citizen.

Herman, raised in poverty and in love, learned responsibility early. At nine he sold newspapers on street corners and walked beside the railroad track to collect pieces of coal for the family stove. Herman saved old newspapers to line his sisters' shoes when their feet were cold. How he longed to lighten his family's burden. He promised himself that one day he would help make their lives easier. Young Herman didn't realize that his ready smile, his clear, strong laugh, and his warm affection already sweetened their lives, and always would.

When Herman was twelve the Lisses moved from New London to New Haven, where Jacob worked in his son-in-law's grocery on Commercial Street. The family joined a new synagogue, the Bikur Chalem Shul, an Orthodox house of worship devoted to study, prayer, and charity.

Herman attended weekly Sabbath services with his mother, he sitting in the men's section and she upstairs with the women. A rabbi came to the home each week to help prepare Herman for his bar mitzvah, the ceremony that would mark his thirteenth birthday and his entrance as an adult into the Jewish faith. On that Sabbath Herman would be called to the pulpit to read from the Torah, the five books of Moses. Herman would then assume the responsibility of fulfilling the commandments. As their brother studied the ancient chants and learned to read and write in Hebrew, the girls sat with him and the rabbi. They listened, and they learned as well.

Excitement swirled in the Liss home in anticipation of Herman's bar mitzvah. Rose sewed his first suit and took him to buy a new shirt and tie, socks and shoes. The thrill of selecting clothes to match his fitted suit cast a deep impression, one that remained with him for a lifetime. Days before the bar mitzvah, Herman's mother and aunts baked strudels and pastries and pies to serve at the celebration that followed the service.

On the Sabbath following Herman's thirteenth birthday, in August 1922, his father lifted the Torah scroll from the ark and lovingly placed it in Herman's arms. From this scroll Herman chanted the words that connected him to his ancestors and to the house of Israel. Herman was a link in a chain of souls, and he chose on that day to honor his faith and responsibilities for all of his life.

Following the service, family and friends crowded into the Liss's small apartment to congratulate Herman and to toast his arrival to manhood. "*L'Chaim*—to Life!" they cheered as they lifted their glasses of wine.

"Thank you. Thank you," smiled the newest member of their community.

HERMAN GREW INTO A YOUNG MAN every parent would wish for a son, every sister a brother, every youth a best friend, and every girl a suitor. By seventeen Herman was over six feet tall, muscular, and strikingly handsome. Kindness was reflected in his clear blue eyes and gentle gaze.

Academically and athletically, Herman excelled in school. Words were his friends, and he envisioned himself a journalist like his hero, Walter Winchell. In the fall of Herman's senior year he was promoted from selling newspapers on the streets of New Haven to manager of the city newsboys. This meant a small increase in salary. He had always given his money to help support his family. Now, his parents insisted that he keep a little each week for himself.

Herman had had his eye on a gray felt fedora, a hat that was popular among the reporters at the *New Haven Union*. By the following spring he had saved enough money—five dollars—to buy a slate fedora with a small feather and a sharp crease. Never had he been more proud. Herman saved that hat for only special occasions. In the late spring he had reason to wear it. The managing editor of the *New Haven Union* asked Herman to supervise a promotional trip to New York for the newsboys. They were going to Yankee stadium to see a game, and for most it was their first excursion out of the city.

Returning home, Herman asked the driver to stop at a roadside store so the boys could be treated to ice cream courtesy of the paper. All thirty rushed into the little shop. Herman stood at the counter as the boys selected their flavors. Licking their cones, the boys surveyed the store. Herman paid and led them back to the bus.

The moment the driver closed the door, the frantic owner charged out of the store, screaming as his arms flailed. Herman jumped off the bus to talk to him.

"The boys stole from me! They took gum and candy without paying!"

Herman assured him that he would take care of the situation.

"Excuse me for a minute, and I'll be back with whatever the boys took. I'm so sorry."

The owner returned to the store shaking his head. Herman turned to speak to his charges.

"Boys," he said. "Some of you made a mistake. You took items and didn't pay. I'm going to pass my hat around the bus, and I will stay up front and turn my back. Whatever you took, please put back in the hat. No questions will be asked."

The hat was passed from boy to boy starting at the front of the bus. By the time it came back on the other side, it was full—full of empty candy wrappers, chewed gum, and chocolate spit.

Herman paid the owner out of his own pocket.

In June 1928 Herman graduated from high school. He delivered stacks of newspapers to the boys, morning and evening, and managed the accounts. In his free time Herman practiced the journalism skills he learned in class and working on the school paper. Anxious to become a cub reporter, Herman planned to present his columns to the managing editor in the fall.

In early November an interview was arranged. The young candidate earnestly presented his request. "I'll be happy to write local stories, anything, please. I just want a chance to become a journalist."

The editor had been impressed by Herman's performance in the past year. "I tell you what, son. We could use someone to attend our New Haven boxing matches, write a few lines, and then transmit them by Teletype to the United Press. I'd like you to continue working with our kids, too. You'll earn a few extra bucks, get some experience, and next Thanksgiving we can talk about a position for you."

"Thank you, thank you!" Herman pumped the editor's hand as his heart danced. At nineteen he had his entrée into the world of journalism.

After every local fight Herman returned to the office late at night, wrote his 100 words, and sent them over the wires. Herman slept only a few hours before having to awake to drop off the morning papers. Although sleep deprived, his energy swelled. Herman knew that he was getting close to a position as a full-fledged reporter. He could feel it.

On October 23, 1929, when Herman arrived at his desk to write his sports story, there was panic in the newsroom. The next morning's headline read "Disaster on Wall Street! Banks Fail!" The stock market had crashed and people flooded the banks, pulling out their life savings. Banks closed while depositors stood in line. Former millionaires jumped from hotel windows.

Herman, at twenty, lost his job at the *New Haven Union*. Customers no longer had a nickel to spend on newspapers.

The Lisses needed Herman's salary to survive, but there were no jobs. He began to work for his brother-in-law at the Quality Cut Rate Market, the store where his father sold vegetables. Sawdust covered the floor, and a pot-bellied stove provided heat. Herman worked the register, which was filled with more chits than change. He cleaned the bins, set up the displays, and made the signs. He also delivered the groceries. The powerful young man carried heavy boxes down busy city streets and up long flights of stairs. He worked fourteen hours a day, six days a week.

One late winter night as Herman trudged up to the top of a four-story building balancing cartons of groceries, he tripped on a child's toy left on the stairs. He lost his footing and fell backward. Cans of food tumbled after him as he slid down the stairs. Breathless, Herman lay on the darkened landing. A searing pain shot through his back as he pulled himself up on the railing. Slowly, hunched over, he gathered the cans, and sitting on each stair, moved the groceries up, one step at a time. Herman made his delivery and, still bent, crept home.

For ten years Herman worked with his father and brother-in-law. A favorite with customers, he became the assistant manager and buyer for the market. The food salesmen pitched their new products to Herman for his approval. He found himself mesmerized by the art of sales and studied the techniques and styles of these business people. Herman analyzed their manner and their dress, the way they conducted themselves. It was then that Herman recognized that "a man sells himself before he sells his product." One day, he promised himself, he, too, would become a successful salesman.

Herman, now in his late twenties, was a very popular young man. On Saturday nights he attended dances where his natural rhythm and grace, in concert with his charm, made him a most desirable partner. The young women followed Herman with their eyes and murmured silent prayers that he would invite them to dance. When the band began to play, Herman's body swayed and his foot tapped. He couldn't stay still. As new dances became crazes, Herman watched those few who had the time and the money to take lessons. With a little practice, he, too, learned the steps. Dancing was in his soul and in his cells.

One May afternoon when Herman was thirty, his father Jacob died suddenly. In anguish, the close family turned to Herman for strength. Herman turned to God. He attended synagogue services twice a day, morning and evening, to say *Kaddish* for his father, the mourner's prayer. Traditionally, the prayer is said for a parent for eleven months, seven days a week. Herman missed not one day. During that time, mourners refrain from entertainment and music and dance. Respect for his father's memory was absolute.

HERMAN WAS NOW THE SOLE SUPPORT of his mother. He and Rose lived together in a small apartment. His three older sisters were married and had their own families. Rose longed to see her son with a wife, wishing for his happiness and for a grandchild to carry on the family name. But after the mourning period Herman's life became even richer than before, and he wasn't ready to think about marriage. Promoted to store manager, Herman delighted in his work, weekend dances, and Sundays at the beach with good friends. A wedding could wait!

On December 7, 1941, six months after Herman's life returned to normal, disaster struck. Pearl Harbor was attacked, and the world plunged into war. Many of Herman's friends enlisted in the service, and he, too, wanted to fight for his country. Herman told Rose his plans.

"No, Chaim, please don't go! Your father just died, and you are my only son. Please don't do this! Not now!"

Herman was torn. His family still had relatives in Poland, and there was news of Jews being ripped from their homes and tortured and gassed in concentration camps. Now America had been attacked. How could he do nothing?

Reluctantly, Herman honored his mother's pleas, but by late in 1942 he was drafted into the army. Rose was inconsolable. She cried out again and again, "God, please, save my child!"

On the day of Herman's induction, Rose visited the rabbi. She clutched her son's picture to her.

"Rabbi, I am so afraid," she cried in Yiddish. "Herman is leaving for the war today, and I am frightened that I may never see him again."

"Mrs. Liss, you must have faith. Herman will be safe. He will not carry a gun into war."

The rabbi's words did little to reassure Rose. He was a rabbi, not a seer. How could he know the future or the pain in her heart? The message seemed absurd, almost patronizing. Rose left as heartsick as she came.

Herman reported for boot camp at Fort Devens, Massachusetts. For weeks he marched, dug foxholes, crawled on his belly carrying a heavy pack, jumped over barricades, and learned to fire a gun. In the spring of 1943 he received his orders. He was to be deployed to Europe on a convoy sailing from New York. The night before his departure he packed his duffel bag and prepared his rifle. Along with his gear Herman placed the prayer book his parents had given him on the day of his bar mitzvah, twenty years earlier.

Before the sun rose the battalion of soldiers marched onto the train that was to carry them from Boston to New York. Herman bent down to lift his bulging pack to the shelf above his head. As he raised the sack and pushed it forward, a piercing pain shot through his back. His muscles went into spasm, and he couldn't stand. Herman remembered that vise-like grip. He saw himself lying on a darkened landing at the bottom of a long flight of stairs.

Herman was taken by ambulance to an infirmary in New York where he was diagnosed with a chronic back condition related to his fall. Marching, lifting, digging, jumping, crawling induced the spasm. Herman would not be allowed to go to Europe. He would not carry a gun into war.

Corporal Herman Liss served his country on American soil. Stationed in Virginia, Colorado, and Washington, he used his skills on the telegraph to receive, send, and interpret military messages.

Ironically, though, Herman could not communicate directly with his own mother, who was unable to read English. Rose went to the synagogue each day to thank God for sparing her son. She prayed for the safety of all of the sons and for the end of the horrors in Europe.

Herman had an idea. Although Rose didn't read English and Herman didn't know how to write in Yiddish, he would ask his sisters to send him the phonetic equivalents of the Hebrew alphabet, the language in which Yiddish was written. Herman could write to his mother in Yiddish, his first language, and spell the words phonetically. He broke the code.

In 1945 Herman received his honorable discharge and returned to a jubilant homecoming. At thirty-six he was prepared to begin life anew, to follow his heart. Herman challenged himself to earn a living as a salesman—the salesman he envisioned while he was in the service.

Herman dressed in his finest blue suit, highly polished black leather shoes, and red, white, and blue-striped tie. His hair was freshly cut and his nails trimmed and clean. He was to interview for a sales position with Educator Biscuit Company, a bakery that sold to stores throughout New England. When the interviewer entered the room, Herman rose to his full height, extended his hand, smiled, and held the man's gaze. The job was his even before he said a word.

Herman was hired to travel to stores from Maine through Rhode Island, selling cookies and crackers for the well-known manufacturer. His enthusiasm and dedication propelled him into the position of regional manager within a year. During the week Herman worked feverishly. His own sales continued to mount, and he inspired others whom he managed to boost their profits. Soon his team outpaced all the others.

On the weekends Herman played just as hard. He and his bachelor friends frequented resorts in the Catskill Mountains of New York and in Connecticut. At Grossinger's and Brown's and Kutcher's and Banner Lodge, he played tennis and basketball and swam. And oh, how he danced! The eligible young women fell hard for Herman, and one after another invited him to meet their parents. Their fathers, hoping to entice Herman to marry their daughters, tried to tempt him with promises of executive positions and shares in their companies. But Herman was not for sale. Not for any price!

Rose, meanwhile, was fulfilling her own cherished dream. She applied to the New Haven Public Evening School, and for two years studied in preparation for citizenship. She learned to read and write and understand the workings of our government. At sixty-six, Rose became an American.

Herman began to receive recognition and awards for his sales acumen. Competing companies became aware of his talents, and he was offered positions by regional and national food concerns. But Herman was devoted to the company that gave him his start, and he remained with them for twenty years, until they were sold.

Offers from other companies began to arrive, and Herman thoughtfully considered each one. He wanted to remain in New Haven, where he and Rose lived. Rose was ill, and he wished to stay close. Lopes Associates, a family owned regional Italian food distributor, presented Herman with an opportunity to manage a sales force in New England. They promised him that when necessary he could take the time to care for his mother. They would also provide him with a brand new company car each year. Best of all, Herman could assemble his own team and use his creativity without restriction. Would he please give them a chance? He did, and from 1965 until his retirement fifteen years later, Herman Liss and his sales force broke company records.

In May 1968, thirty years to the day that Jacob died, Rose passed away. A light was extinguished for Herman. Just as he had for his father, Herman attended the synagogue twice a day, every day, to say *Kaddish* in his mother's memory. For eleven months Herman worked and prayed. That was all he did.

When the mourning period ended, Harry, a friend of Herman's, invited him to a gathering in New York of the newly formed Business and Professional Singles Association.

"I really don't feel like socializing yet," protested Herman.

"Oh, come on. You know your mother wouldn't want you to live like a hermit. *You're* still alive!"

Herman grudgingly went with Harry. They drove together to New Rochelle for a dinner party sponsored by the BPSA. Herman felt distant, removed from the chatter and joviality of the evening. As they prepared to leave, a woman approached him.

"Hi, my name is Eva. Thank you for coming tonight. We hope that you'll want to join us and become a member."

Herman recognized Eva as the president of the club, the officer who had welcomed the gathering before the meal. He thanked her, introduced himself, and shook her hand.

"Herman," Eva continued, "We're looking for people to chair a few of our committees. I wonder if you might consider helping me plan some of our upcoming events?"

Herman smiled politely, if not enthusiastically. He felt a poke in his back. Harry answered for him. "How would you like us to co-chair your committee? I'll see to it that Herman gets here!"

"That would be wonderful. Our next planning session is at the end of the month, in two weeks."

"We'll be here," called Harry as he grabbed Herman's arm. "See you in two weeks!"

"What did you do that for?" challenged Herman as they got into the car.

"Come on, Herman, live a little!"

FOR THE NEXT YEAR HERMAN, Harry, and Eva met monthly to plan parties, dances, lectures, and excursions for the Business and Professional Singles Association of Greater New York. Eva, a widow, was wildly attracted to Herman. She made certain that they sat together at all of the events, and soon they were seeing each other nearly every week. Herman was becoming fond of this intelligent, dynamic lady.

"Herman," Eva said to him one evening when they were at her home. "You're going to be sixty soon, and I'm not getting any younger. We're both living alone, and I know we could be good together. I love you, and I hope you feel the same. Why don't we get married?"

Herman and Eva wed in the summer of 1969 in a temple in New Rochelle. After a honeymoon in Jamaica, they settled into an apartment midway between New York and New Haven. Herman was content. Their love was comfortable and companionable and warmed them.

Herman commuted to his work in New Haven and Eva to hers in New York. It was a long drive for them both, and by the winter Eva's interminable energy began to flag. She grew pale and weak. Perhaps it was the job or the drive or the many recent changes in her life, they reasoned. Eva took some time from work and rested. But she did not improve. A cough, mild at first, grew more insistent. She began to lose weight.

Herman convinced his wife to see her doctor. The physician was shocked at her rapid decline. He examined Eva and sent her for blood tests and X-rays. Within days the doctor called and asked Eva to return with Herman.

"I'm sorry," began the doctor. "Eva, your X-rays show lesions on both of your lungs. We need to do a biopsy right away. That will tell us more."

The following day Eva entered the hospital for surgery. The biopsy results were more serious than the doctor had imagined. She had advanced melanoma—skin cancer that had metastasized throughout her body. There was no treatment. She hadn't long to live.

Herman took Eva home and gently, lovingly cared for her. A few months later, on their first anniversary, Eva died.

HERMAN STOOD AT THE GRAVE as Eva's casket was lowered into the ground next to Jacob and Rose. He glanced at the empty plot beside his wife. It was covered with the fresh mound of dirt that would blanket Eva's coffin, topping the earth that would eventually cover him. The mourner's prayer sprang from his lips. *"Yisgadal V'yiskadash Shmae Rahbah—"* Herman cried.

Each morning and evening, just as he had for his parents, Herman went to the temple to pray, this time for his wife. Often Herman led the service, and with the other congregants read Psalm 30. They recited together, "Weeping may linger for the night; but joy comes with the dawn."

Herman could not then imagine that one day the light would return.

BETTY LEAVITT—A LIGHT

IN 1919, WHEN HERMAN WAS NINE AND LIVING IN THE seaside town of New London, Connecticut, an infant was born up the coast in Revere, Massachusetts.

Betty Leavitt burst into life in the midst of a wild February 12th snowstorm. The obstetrician was also the mayor of Revere. He was conducting town business when word came that Lillian was in labor. By the time the physician's horse slipped and sloshed through the snow to arrive at 222 North Shore Road, Betty had made her entrance. Racing up the stairs, the doctor found a healthy suckling infant with a full head of black hair topped by a bright red ribbon. Betty's grandfather, loving and superstitious, had pinned it there for the protection of this irrepressible gift.

Betty's entrances were always full of flair. Her light and laughter were contagious, and other children and adults were drawn to her spark. Betty's Russian immigrant parents, Max and Lillian, fostered their child's curiosity, confidence, and loving nature. They provided her with lessons in elocution, dance, and piano. Betty despised the tap and enforced music practice, but adored learning and reciting poetry and fanciful stories. Soon she was creating her own.

Betty grew into an enticing little girl who dazzled teachers and classmates with her imagination. She entertained with stories, impersonations, and delicious humor. The tallest in her class, Betty was also the quickest in mind and body.

The Leavitts were part of a small, closely knit Jewish community just north of Boston. Revere was populated principally by large Italian and Irish families who worked hard to provide their children with the American dream. Betty's parents, too, wanted her and her older brother, Sam, to thrive in this amazing new land. Together they worked and saved to open a small men's clothing store on Shirley Avenue. Betty was enthralled as her parents decorated the store windows and assisted customers with their purchases. She watched and learned and began mesmerizing patrons with her natural sales ability. They couldn't refuse an eight-year-old who could match shirts and ties and belts!

On weekends Betty and Sam would accompany their parents to the homes of aunts, uncles, cousins, and friends. Their visits were filled with music, dance, abundant food, and a sweet sense of community.

Late one Saturday evening, when it was Max and Lillian's turn to entertain, there was a loud banging on the door. It was the police. Their store had burned to the ground.

Betty's parents decided to start a new life right on Revere Beach— the oldest public beach in the nation, featuring a crescent-shaped, mile-long swath of sand caressed by tumbling waves. Revere Beach was home to amusement rides, dance halls, carnival tents, and food stands. The family purchased a two-story white stucco home at 395 Revere Beach Boulevard and built an attached refreshment stand directly across from the beach. Ocean View Café was born.

MAX AND LILLIAN, SAM AND BETTY sold hot dogs, hamburgers, clam fritters, popcorn, peanuts, and ice cream to swimmers and sun worshippers from early spring through the autumn. The days were long and the work intense, but together the family was able to create a thriving business. When the throngs of beach-goers thinned, Betty would hear the *ching* of the cash register and Max would hand his daughter a few coins for the Ferris wheel or merry-go-round, the Cyclone, the salt-water pool, Bluebeard's Palace or the Fun House.

The move to their new home meant a change of school for Betty in the third grade. She was the only new child in her class, and on the first day was approached by another student who said, "Doris Grinell wants to meet you in the recess yard after school." Betty sensed that this was not a welcoming party. She was right.

When the dismissal bell rang, Betty was met in the back by a yard full of feisty kids. Doris marched up to her and hollered, "OK. I'm the class boss. You got that?" She began to pummel Betty.

What Doris didn't know was that Betty had honed her wrestling and pugilistic skills on her big brother Sam, three years older.

The other children took up the chant "Yay, Doris! Yay, Doris!" Hearing that, Betty jumped on Doris, knocking her to the ground. Betty punched her, sat on her, and screamed, "Say Uncle, Doris! Say Uncle!"

Quietly at first, and then louder, the other children chorused "Yay, Betty! Yay, Betty!" She could barely hear Doris's concession over their squeals.

The next day Betty's classmates brought her marbles and penny candy. She never had to fight again.

THE OCEAN WAS BETTY'S BEST FRIEND. Its tides coursed through her veins, sung to her, lifted and soothed her. She couldn't resist its salty call.

One early spring afternoon, on a walk home from third grade, her friend beckoned. The sun sparkled like white diamonds on the cobalt sea. Betty knew the warning about swimming alone, but the pull was too great. She placed her books on the sand, yanked off her shoes and socks, and waded in. *I'll just walk up to my ankles,* the eight-year-old assured herself. *No one will know.*

The waves crooked their jeweled fingers. Now up to her knees, she lifted her skirt. It wasn't enough. Betty dove and jumped and splashed and swam. She sensed that this forbidden swim would be the sweetest of her life. Whatever the punishment, it was worth it.

Chilled by the cold water and cool wind, Betty shivered as she ran home. "I didn't mean it!" she cried when her mother opened the door.

Lillian took a look at her soaking wet child, wrapped her in a thirsty towel, and hugged her close.

The wonder of that afternoon remained with Betty always.

BETTY'S INNOCENCE, SECURITY, and carefree days, like the trolley that ran to Revere Beach, came to a screeching halt. In 1929 the Depression slammed the country.

People were destitute. They no longer had money to spend on carnival rides and clam rolls. By the time Betty was twelve, their home and business were gone. The seaside house, filled with so much love and laughter, was taken over by the bank. As the furniture was being removed for auction, Betty ran upstairs to her closet and on the wall wrote, "I love you house."

The little family moved to a chilly one-room bungalow in the back of a cousin's home. It had an outside shower and latrine. There were just two beds—Betty slept with her mother and Sam with his father. The little family worked, when they could, for relatives who still owned stands on the beach. Lillian sold hosiery from their tiny apartment, but their efforts were not enough to keep their bellies full. Poverty forced them more than once to hock the treasured silver samovar that Lillian had carried on the boat from Russia. The cherished piece gleamed not in their kitchen, but in someone else's store window. One day it would become the centerpiece in Betty's own home and then in my own.

In the midst of scarcity, Betty grew to be over 5'10" tall. Her beauty and verve were as impressive as her height. She was a class leader as well as class comic, although so clever that it was her friends, not she, who would be chastised for her antics. Betty often whispered asides during lectures at Garfield Junior High and then at Revere High School. When the teachers saw her neighbors laughing, they'd say, "Don't bother Miss Leavitt! Why are you laughing at her?" The out-of-control classmates would be sent to the back of the room as Betty maintained her poise.

On the day of Betty's high school graduation the family moved from Revere to Hartford, Connecticut, where her married brother now lived. Betty sobbed as friends, waving and crying, encircled the car. Her own bed, a warm bath, and enough to eat were one hundred miles from her beloved beach. It felt like an ocean away.

Striking and smart, Betty soon found work as a bookkeeper and was often invited by colleagues and friends to dances and parties and dinners. Very discriminating, and enjoying her own company and that of her parents, she often gracefully declined. One Sunday when Betty was twenty, her cousins drove her to meet some friends who owned a dairy farm. There she was introduced to other visitors—a man and a woman and a young child.

The next evening Betty received a call. "Hello, Betty, This is Morris. We met yesterday at the farm. I'm wondering if you would consider going out to dinner with me this Saturday?"

"I don't go out with married men!" Betty shot back.

"Married—I'm not married."

"Well, who was that woman and child you were with?"

Morris laughed. "They are my sister and my niece. Now will you go to dinner with me?"

"How did you get my number?"

"I copied down the license plate number on the car and went to the motor vehicle office. They gave me your cousin's phone number, and he gave me yours."

Betty was impressed by this man's resourcefulness. She agreed to meet him for dinner and found him to be intelligent, sensitive, and kind. They dated for a year, fell in love, and were engaged just before Pearl Harbor was attacked.

Morris enlisted in the navy and was in Europe on a transport ship for nearly four years manning guns and the supply room. Several times the berths where his ship was docked were bombed just minutes before his Large Ship Transport arrived or soon after it sailed.

When Morris returned from the war in January 1945, Betty was twenty-five and he thirty. They honored their promise to marry as quickly as possible. Standing under the wedding canopy in their new apartment on Garden Street in Hartford, Betty could not have known that Morris was different than the man she remembered. On the honeymoon in New York she had hints that her new husband was plagued by depression and anxiety, punctuated by irrational fears.

Two years later I was born, and nearly three years after that I had a baby brother, Barry. By the time Barry came, Morris's depression gave way to paranoia, darkening his days and shading my parents' marriage.

BETTY WORKED WITH MORRIS in the office of a manufacturing plant to provide the crutch he needed to function. She came home with him, spent every day and every night with him, trying to keep our little family safe and together. Even in the midst of Morris's darkest hours, my mother held the light for all of us. She raised my brother and myself and took care of her widowed mother, who lived with us. Mom taught us by example what it meant to respect, support, and cherish a parent. She cared for my grandmother as though she were her precious child, just as my grandmother had cared for her own mother.

For Betty, keeping our world stable in spite of my father's mental illness demanded enormous stamina and creativity. I remember as an eight-year-old pleading with my father to remove the training wheels from my bike. "I'm the only kid on the block who still has those baby wheels!" I cried.

"No," he answered, time and time again. "You could fall and get hurt."

Mom asked a neighbor to take them off.

As a teen-ager I needed to practice driving in preparation for my license. "You might get into an accident!" my father warned.

It was my mother who got her license and then took me out.

BETTY WAS NEVER the Betty Crocker, Florence Nightingale, Martha Stewart kind of mom. No, she was more an amalgam of Peter Pan, Auntie Mame, and the Pied Piper. Her zest bubbled over and made life juicy.

One Saturday morning when I was about twelve and my brother nine, we woke to find that there was very little in the refrigerator. It had been a busy week at work, my father had been especially down, and there just hadn't been time to shop. Barry and I took a look at the lone orange, a couple of pieces of bread, and a little butter that sat alone on the top shelf. As we turned to our mother to complain, Mom's eyes began to sparkle.

In her best Parisian accent she suggested, "Let's make this a French breakfast!" With a flourish she served us *l'orange, le pain,* and *le beurre,* fortifying us with life and laughter.

It is the only breakfast of the thousands of our growing up years that my brother and I still remember. Mom may not have been Julia Child, but she taught us to savor life.

There were glorious surprises, too. Once or twice a year, while it was still dark, Mom would wake us and say, "Get up, get dressed, we're going to New York!" We'd take a train from Hartford to Manhattan and on arrival stop for theater tickets at the discount theater booth on Broadway. Before lunch we'd visit the Metropolitan Museum of Art, where we learned to love color and design and form. Mom would take us to the cafeteria with tables placed around a pool complete with classical fountain sculpture. The beauty and the joy were so great that

I couldn't eat.

After a visit to my favorite gallery, the Impressionist exhibit, we'd leave for the theater or a show at Radio City Music Hall. When my brother and I became teenagers, Mom would take us individually to give us her full attention, and I think to spare herself our incessant teasing. Those days alone with her were the sweetest.

When I was sixteen, my mother took me for my first overnight in New York. The smash hit *Fiddler On the Roof* had just opened, and it was sold out for months. When we got off the train and went into the little shop for tickets, the man asked, "What would you like to see today?"

"Fiddler on the Roof," Betty announced.

"Lady, you've got to be kidding. That would take a miracle!"

"I believe in miracles," Mom replied.

"In that case, come back here at 6:00, and I'll see what I can do. But no promises."

We returned to his store that evening and he handed us two tickets to *Fiddler On The Roof*, third row center, aisle seats. Mom not only believed in miracles, she invited them!

BETTY'S DEAREST DREAM was to travel, but Morris was petrified of change. She used to say, "One day, I'm going to the seashore!" I'd affirm, "I know you will!"

In my mid-teens, my brother and I begged my father to take us to Nova Scotia, an island off the eastern coast of Canada. He agreed that for our summer vacation, several months away, we'd drive to Bar Harbor, Maine and from there take the ferry on to our destination. For weeks my mother, brother, and I dreamt about this trip, and the night before our July departure the three of us packed the car. We laughed and sang as we arranged the luggage. Morris paced the floor.

The next morning we hurriedly dressed and ran down the stairs. My father, now frantically pacing the house in his underwear, announced, "We can't go. I can't take time off from work. I have too much to do."

My brother and I couldn't believe it. I was feeling especially hurt for my mother, while she was agonizing about our disappointment.

"I've got a week off from work, kids, and we're not going to waste it! Let's get our things out of the car and repack. How would you like to go to the World's Fair? There are buses going from Hartford to the New York Fairgrounds, and I'll call and see if we can get a hotel reservation. You'll see, we'll have fun!"

Mom, Barry and I spent three incredible days at the 1964 World's Fair. Each day we returned to visit the centerpiece of the fair, Michelangelo's *Pieta*. The rest of the week we stayed in New London, Connecticut at Ocean Beach. The three of us laughed and played in the ocean, my brother and I grateful to have our mother to ourselves. We'd arrive at the beach early in the morning and spend the entire day reveling in the sun and sea and sand. At sunset Mom would point at the golden yolk dipping below the hot-pink and purple horizon. She'd enthuse, "Look at that. Isn't this spectacular?" Then Betty would clap her hands and cheer, "Yay, God!"

Mom was not a traditionally religious woman, but she had a personal and passionate relationship with God. Although my parents enrolled my brother and myself in Hebrew School, and our family attended holiday services, Mom's preference was to pray at home or on the beach. She'd say, "I love being Jewish, but I don't have to go to a building to pray."

There was no dogma, no fear of God—just pure reverence for the Divine, her fellow man, and nature. Mom's was a lived faith. She shared generously and made the other feel worthy, special. "An educated mind is important," she'd often say. "But more important, still, is an educated heart."

BETTY WAS A FASHION MAVEN who adored color and style. And how she loved to coordinate her clothes and accessories. A child of the Depression, Betty valued bargains. When she saw an outfit she liked and felt it was too expensive, she'd either wait for it to go on sale or find that style elsewhere at a better price. Shopping with her was an adventure. First she'd see a gorgeous outfit, then look at the price tag, and would most often say in Yiddish—so that no one else would understand—"*Nisht Natik.*" Not Necessary. That meant we'd find it at a better price. She usually did.

Betty gave birth to two children, but was mother to so many more. From the time I was a child through my adult years, my friends adopted Betty as their own. In elementary school a classmate who lived in an orphanage came home with me every week and pretended that Mom was her mother, too. In college my dormmates would visit Betty on weekends when I stayed at school. They just wanted to be with a mother who knew how to love unconditionally, listen intently, and laugh with abandon. My friends called her Mom.

Betty was hysterically funny, and I always felt that I was running to keep up with her. We teased each other endlessly—gales of laughter washing over and through us, my mind sharpened against her brilliant wit. I remember one day telling her with great disbelief that a friend's relative willed her body to the local medical school for dissection rather than pay for a burial. Mom shot back, "Oh, Frieda, may she rest in pieces!"

BETTY'S RAZOR-SHARP HUMOR was an incredible survival tool. It helped her maintain her sanity through the years that Morris was losing his. Shortly before their twenty-third anniversary, my father was hospitalized with a major breakdown. He received more electric shock treatment, another change of medication, and intense therapy. Discharged after several weeks, Morris was fired from his work.

Now, with a daughter grown and married and a son in college, Mom knew it was time for her to leave the job where she and my father had worked for so many unhappy years. She applied for the position of administrative assistant to the Director of Psychiatry of the Connecticut State Drug and Alcohol Division. Betty took the state exam and was hired the next week. Her job was filled with challenge and stimulation. She flourished.

Morris was hospitalized again a few months after she began her new career. Betty recognized that if she stayed with my father much longer, her own life would be in jeopardy. It was time to file for divorce—time for her to leave, time for her to live.

The next two years were tumultuous. Morris contested the divorce, and there was a court battle. It was the only contested divorce in Connecticut in 1970. Betty now lived alone, and although burdened by the legal wrangling and endless expenses, she didn't give up.

During her summer vacation Betty traveled to Nova Scotia with a dear friend, making the trip that was denied her five years earlier. There she bought her first small oil painting, a vibrant floral bouquet. As we were growing up, my mother often recited the saying, "If you have two pennies, with the first buy bread, and with the second buy hyacinths for your soul."

Mom was feeding her soul, and the best of days were yet ahead.

THE DANCE

HERMAN AND BETTY BOTH BECAME SINGLE IN 1970—he through death, she divorce. Betty at fifty shone with a fresh glow now that she could be her full self. Men were enchanted by her, yet not one captivated this sparkling spirit. Betty met lots of men, but generally she'd say about her dates, "Well, Stella thinks he's good looking," or "Rita says he's a successful business-man. They can have him!"

Very selective, Mom preferred to stay at home and read a good book rather than waste her time with someone she considered dull. "Please," she teased, "don't ever let me get so desperate as to say 'yes' just to be married!" I promised her I wouldn't.

After nearly two years of dating and more than one proposal, my mother called to say, "I met a man yesterday." Never before did she lead with those words or sound so breathless.

PRINCE CHARMING LIVED ONLY in fairy tales—or so Betty believed until Herman strode across a dance floor and held out his hand to her.

"May I have this dance?" asked the Prince.

"Truthfully, I'm not a very good dancer," responded the lovely lady.

"Ah," he assured. "Don't worry. I'm a strong leader."

Herman took Betty in his arms. They fit perfectly together. With his left hand gentle yet firm against her waist and their cheeks touching, Betty and Herman moved with an easy grace.

There was energy—electricity—a spark between them that both of

48

them felt. Neither spoke or wanted to let go at the end of the song, but the music stopped.

Together they walked back to the table and sat down, everyone and everything fading away.

"I'm Herman Liss, and you *are* a good dancer."

"Thank you, Herman. I'm Betty Farber, and you made me look good."

"Have you been to the Forest House before?" asked Herman.

"No, this is the first time. I don't live near here. My friend wanted to come and asked me to keep her company on the trip to upstate New York."

"Where do you live?" asked Herman.

"I live in Connecticut. Bloomfield."

Herman laughed. "I live in Connecticut, too—in New Haven."

"Have you been to the Forest House dances in the past?" asked Betty.

"I used to come on occasion before I was married." Herman paused, "My wife died just a year ago."

"I'm so sorry. This must be hard for you. How long were you married?"

"Only one year. My wife died on our first anniversary." Herman's eyes misted, and he gazed away.

"You must miss her terribly."

"Yes, with all my heart. I never thought I'd marry, and when I did, I believed it would last a lifetime."

The band began to play another slow song and Herman rose. As Herman took Betty into his arms, he said, "I wasn't planning on coming tonight. I really don't feel ready to start going out. My friend Harry called this morning and said he had been planning to come, was going to meet a lady friend here, but his car broke down. He asked me to drive him."

"So we both are here for our friends," laughed Betty.

Herman smiled and held her close.

"Betty," Herman asked, "Do you ever go to the Singles Dances at the Jewish Community Center in West Hartford?"

"The Center's not far from my home, but I've never gone to the dances. Mostly I've been there to swim."

"Well, I've heard that there's a wonderful band there. The dances are held the last Saturday of every month. Harry sometimes goes. Do you think you might try it in September?"

"Maybe I will."

"I hope you do."

THE NEXT MORNING when my mother and I spoke, I held my breath as she described the evening and the man. "Do you think you'll see Herman again, Mom?"

"Well, he asked if I'm going to go to the Singles Dance in West Hartford next month."

"Will he be there?"

"Oh, I hope so!"

The next month was filled with challenging and rewarding work, visits with friends, and dinner and movie dates. Still, Betty's heart and mind replayed the summer evening each time she had a quiet moment. At fifty-two, she felt like a teenager.

The morning of the dance in West Hartford, Betty had her striking silver hair set in a stylish, short bouffant. She had laid out her dress, aquamarine with a collar that rose high in the back, framing her face and highlighting her elegance. A matching satin rose was pinned just above the bodice. In that dress, Betty looked like a queen.

As she entered the hall, her heart raced. It was overwhelming. There were so many people at the tables, standing in small groups against the walls, and dancing to the Big Band music.

What am I doing here? she wondered, as her throat began to tighten.

"What a honey!" enthused a stocky man as he approached her. "How 'bout a dance?" he exhaled. The man was much shorter than she and smelled of onions.

"No, thank you. Not just now," Betty responded.

"OK, later." The man winked, pointed, and walked away.

Then she saw him. Herman was standing in a corner with three women, each vying for his attention. His eyes were scanning the room.

Mom sat down at a table with two women she had recognized. By now her mouth was dry and her hands shaking. She barely heard the music for the pounding in her ears.

He saw her, excused himself, and crossed the dance floor, a warm smile on his generous lips.

"Betty, you came! I was hoping you'd be here. Would you like to dance?"

This time Mom didn't hesitate. She took his arm and walked to the center of the parquet floor. Their eyes met, and Herman pulled her close.

"You look so beautiful," he said.

Betty smiled and thought, *so do you.*

After the song was over, he brought her to a table for two. "Can I get you something to drink?"

"I'd love some white wine, thank you."

"I'll be right back."

Betty remembered the night she met Herman and Stella had asked, "Doesn't he look like the movie star Melvin Douglas?" *Stella was right,* she thought. She watched as men and women eagerly greeted Herman at the bar.

"You know a lot of people here," Betty said when he returned with their drinks.

"Yes, I was a bachelor for most of my life, and I knew many of these people before I was married. I haven't seen them in a couple of years."

"They are obviously very happy to see you."

"It feels so strange to be here. I never thought I'd be doing this again. It took sixty years for me to marry the first time. I really enjoyed being a bachelor, meeting lots of women. I had a great job, and a very happy life. I thought everything was perfect until I met Eva. We fell in love and wanted to settle down. I never imagined I'd lose her after just a year.

"What about you, Betty? Were you ever married?"

"Yes, for twenty-five years. I've been divorced for almost two."

Betty and Herman talked about their families. He shared stories about his three older sisters, his nieces and nephew, and she spoke of her children and grandson.

When they returned to the dance floor the bandleader stopped the music and asked their names. "You look so good together," he announced. "Betty, I see you have a rose on that lovely blue gown." The band began to play "Red Roses For A Blue Lady." At the end of the song, the conductor announced, "From now on, Betty and Herman, this will be your song."

At the end of the evening, Herman said, "Betty, I had a wonderful time tonight. Do you think you'll come again next month?

"Yes, I'd like that," Betty said. "I'd like that very much."

ON THE LAST SATURDAY EVENING in October, Herman was waiting for Betty in the hallway of the Jewish Community Center.

"I'm so happy you decided to come," he said as he took her coat and hung it up for her.

"Well, I'm delighted to see you, too."

They walked into the dance together. The music stopped. The band began to play "Red Roses For A Blue Lady." *This must be how Cinderella felt,* Betty thought,

Herman and Betty talked and danced and laughed together in a rhythm that was both easy and electric. They reminisced about their childhood—Betty's in Revere, Herman's in New London. Descriptions of their work, their homes, their pleasures tumbled over each other's. The two nodded in recognition of stories never heard, yet deeply understood. And oh, how they danced.

Toward the end of the night Rita, Betty's friend, joined them at the table. She had met Herman years ago when he was single. "I'm having a New Year's Eve party at my house. I'd love it if you'd both come."

Herman looked at Betty, saw her smile, and eagerly accepted. "That'll be great. Thank you. I'll be glad to bring the champagne."

Betty responded, "I'll bring hors d'oeuvres and can help you set up." She couldn't believe it. New Year's Eve with Herman Liss!

Herman and Betty danced the final dance that night. As he pulled her to him, Herman whispered in her ear, "I hope to see you here next month. The dance will be on Thanksgiving weekend. Do you think you can come?"

"Yes," answered Betty. "My kids will be here for the holiday, so I'll be in town."

"That's terrific," Herman replied. "Have a wonderful Thanksgiving."

The one thing Betty was hoping he'd ask, he neglected. He didn't ask for her number.

"I DON'T KNOW WHY he doesn't call me between dances," Mom puzzled as we spoke the next morning. "We have so much fun together."

"Tell me more about him, Mom."

"Herman's a gentleman. He's refined. He's smart. He's funny. He's handsome. He's an amazing dancer. I never enjoyed dancing so much in my life! But why doesn't he ask for my phone number? He dances with only me, he's coming to Rita's New Year's Eve party, but he doesn't call. I don't know why!"

"You told me that his wife died a year ago. Maybe he's scared about starting a new relationship."

"Well, truthfully, so am I."

ON NEW YEAR'S EVE 1971, I got to meet Herman. I was at my mother's home when he came to pick her up for the party. I heard the knock and opened the door. Mom had said he was handsome, but he was so much more. This man was impeccably dressed, sporting a sharp navy blue blazer, gray slacks, and a red and navy striped tie. A starched white handkerchief was tucked into his breast pocket. He smelled terrific. And oh, those sparkling blue eyes!

"Please come in," I gasped.

"Thank you," Herman said, with a smile that lit his face and my heart.

He had a camel-colored cashmere coat over one arm and a teddy bear under the other. He extended his hand and smiled. "How do you do. I'm Herman Liss. You must be Michele. Your mother talks about you all the time, and about her beautiful grandson, Scotty. This is for your baby."

He really was Prince Charming!

When my mother walked into the room, Herman's smile grew even brighter. He presented her with a corsage of baby roses. Never had I seen my Mom look more radiant. She took my breath away. Was this a movie or maybe a dream? I was the mother and she the daughter. She's happy—she's happy—she's happy! That's all that mattered.

Mom and Herman continued to meet at the JCC dances once a month, and each time she saw him she was more enthralled—and more baffled. He now had her phone number, yet still he didn't call, didn't ask her out on dates. Betty received phone calls and invitations from other men, and went out, but Herman's was the only call she longed for. Why wasn't he calling, when every time they met it felt like magic?

JANUARY THROUGH JUNE, the last Saturday night of each month, "Red Roses For A Blue Lady" was played each time Herman and Betty danced their first dance. In July Herman waited, as he always did, by the door. It was a steamy night, and in a suit and tie Herman was getting uncomfortable as the minutes ticked by. Where was she? She usually arrived by 8:15—8:20 at the latest. It was 8:30—8:45—9:00. Still no Betty.

Herman got into line to use the outside phone. It was sweltering, and there was a woman in the booth who seemed to be detailing her entire life story. At 9:30 Betty's phone rang.

"Betty, where are you? Aren't you coming? I've been waiting for you."

"Herman, I just returned from New York. I went to visit the kids today."

"Did you have a good time?"

"Yes, I did, but it was a long ride, and I'm exhausted."

"Well, aren't you coming?"

"No, Herman, I'm not."

"But we always meet at the Singles Dance. I drove over an hour to get here. I miss you. I looked forward to seeing you tonight."

"Bullshit," Betty replied.

"What did you say?"

"I said 'Bullshit!' If you miss me so much, why don't you call me?"

"Is it alright if I come over tonight? I'm just a few blocks away."

"No, Herman, not tonight."

EARLY THE NEXT MORNING Betty received a call. "Hi, Betty—this is Herman. May I take you out for dinner this evening?"

It was their first real date.

That night Herman and Betty agreed that meeting at the dances was no longer enough. They began to see each other every weekend. Sundays, when the weather was clear, they'd go to the shore. Both had grown up at the beach, and spending the day swimming and walking along the water's edge was like heaven to them. They shared so many interests—theater and concerts, museums and nature enticed them both. Being quietly together was also a gift. Each time I called our conversation was about Herman and Betty's adventures. My mother grew even more radiant as the joy and sweetness and connection deepened.

In February of the following year, Herman made Betty a fifty-fifth birthday party at Rita's house, the home where they celebrated their first New Year's Eve. He had come to Rita's early that morning to put up signs he had made and to hang crepe paper and decorations. Herman had arranged for the catering, brought the wine, and sent out the invitations.

Betty introduced Herman to our son, who had just turned three. "Scotty, I'd like you to meet Grandma's special friend, Uncle Herman."

Scott, who couldn't pronounce several of his letters, said, "Oo don't ook ike no uncu to me. Oo ook ike a Gampa."

Herman blushed.

At the end of the evening, when Mom thanked Herman for his kindness—for making her birthday memorable and full of joy—he responded, "You're welcome, sweetheart. It makes me happy to see you so happy."

My heart melted.

THE NEXT SATURDAY NIGHT was the Annual Valentine Ball at the Jewish Community Center. It was a formal dance, black tie for the men, long gowns for the ladies. Herman liked nothing better than to dress in a tuxedo. He would spit-shine his black Italian leather shoes and select his tie and cummerbund several days in advance. Over the years, Herman had acquired quite a collection.

Mom, too, was excited about this event. She bought a stunning light pink gossamer gown with a delicate sequined top. Her shoes were dyed to match the dress. Betty's hair appointment was scheduled for the morning. She felt like a girl getting ready for the prom.

Herman, carrying a wrist corsage, knocked on Betty's door. Betty took a deep breath and peeked through the hole in the door. Even that small glimpse made her head light. She opened the door, and Herman's jaw dropped.

His silver-haired beauty was now light blonde. They stood and stared at each other, their smiles speaking for them.

When Herman and Betty entered the hall, she on his arm, it felt like a dream for both of them. Heads turned as they passed. While they acknowledged the glances and greetings of friends, their eyes and hearts were only for each other.

Toward the end of the evening, as they danced, holding each other close, the singer crooned the lines of a popular song, "May I have this dance for the rest of my life?"

Herman sang in Betty's ear, "May I have this dance for the rest of my life?"

"Are you singing to me—or is this a proposal?" laughed Betty.

Herman stopped dancing, took Betty's hands in his, and gazed into her eyes. "Sweetheart, I want you to be my partner—my only partner. And I want to be yours for the rest of our lives. Will you marry me?"

"Yes, oh yes! I want to be your partner, now and always."

Betty understood then that Herman was her Prince, for real.

THE WEDDING

MY PHONE RANG AT MIDNIGHT.

"Honey, everything is fine. Herman and I have wonderful news!" Together they chorused, "We're engaged!"

I heard the wonder in their voices. At sixty-four and fifty-five, they knew from the depth of their beings the miracle of their love.

My heart leapt. "*Mazel Tov!* Congratulations!" I cheered. "Welcome to our family, Herman. The two of you are meant to be together. Have you thought about a wedding date?"

"How does August 18th sound? It's Herman's 65th birthday!"

"What a gift!"

This was perfect. My husband was finishing medical school in June, and we were moving back to Connecticut for his residency. I could help plan the wedding. At twenty-six, I felt like the Mother of the Bride.

WE HAD SIX MONTHS to get ready. Betty and Herman first needed to find a rabbi to marry them. Herman hoped that his own Orthodox spiritual leader would officiate. My mother was not a member of any synagogue, and she eagerly agreed to be married in the New Haven shul. But there was a problem. On meeting with the rabbi, they were asked if Betty had been married before. She explained that she was divorced after twenty-five years.

"I'll need to see the Jewish divorce decree signed by your husband," the Rabbi said.

"My former husband refused to sign one," Betty explained. "He did not want the civil divorce and contested it in the court. A rabbi and my lawyer tried to contact Morris numerous times to ask him to sign papers for a Jewish divorce, but he hung up. The papers were sent for him to sign, and he ignored them. The rabbi arranged for me to appear before the Conservative Jewish Court in New York and explain my situation. I requested a Jewish divorce based on my civil divorce and documented repeated refusals to respond to the rabbi, the lawyer, or myself. The Conservative Council granted a Jewish divorce, and I have the decree with me." Betty showed the rabbi the document.

He shook his head. "I'm really sorry. I would like to marry you, but I can't. According to Orthodox practice, this divorce is not valid because the husband did not sign it. There is nothing I can do."

Herman shook the rabbi's hand and thanked him. Mom was in tears. "I know how much you want to be married in an Orthodox synagogue," she cried.

"Let's speak to the Orthodox rabbis in your area. Maybe one of them will agree."

They made appointments with several different Orthodox rabbis in Hartford. Each apologized and said that their hands were tied.

"You have a Conservative divorce," Herman said. "We'll find a Conservative rabbi to marry us."

"You would do that?" Betty asked. "You would agree to be married in a Conservative synagogue?"

"Yes, of course—I love you, and I want you to be my wife. We'll find a way!"

UNDERSTANDING AND RESPECT became the lifeblood of Betty and Herman's relationship. As the weeks turned into months, they continued to discover shared values despite dissimilar experiences and expectations. Humor and commitment peppered their debates, and together they designed solutions for their future.

Jewish dietary laws, lighting the Sabbath candles, and synagogue attendance were sacred to Herman. He was raised in a traditional home where milk and meat were not eaten together, dairy and meat dishes were kept separate, and shellfish and pork were forbidden.

Betty, who revered God and was proud of her Judaism, was more spiritual than observant. She had never kept kosher, and synagogue attendance was infrequent. Fried clams were her favorite treat, and pizza with sausage and cheese was a staple. Melding their lives would take patience, understanding, and lots of love.

Mom promised to keep a kosher home, and Herman would teach her how. He agreed that when they went out to eat she was free to order whatever she wished, lobster included. Betty committed to lighting the Sabbath candles, and they decided that Herman would continue to attend services without expecting Betty to accompany him. Major holidays would be celebrated together in the synagogue.

Religious differences weren't their only ones. Herman, a food sales-man, was addicted to supermarkets. He loved to food shop, and the preparation for the weekly event was almost as thrilling to him as the high he got in the aisles. Clipping coupons on Sunday night was a ritual, and comparing food prices in the weekend fliers was a science involving lists and cross checks.

Betty despised shopping. She had memories of racing through the market after work, buying food for a family of five while planning din-ner. As she filled the cart Morris paced the aisles, urging her to hurry.

It was agreed that Herman would do the shopping.

WHILE CREATING THE GROUNDWORK for a new life together, Betty and Herman found a Conservative rabbi who embraced them. He joyfully worked with the couple to design their wedding ceremony.

In late July Betty and Herman visited the town hall to apply for the license. They approached the window hand in hand, excited and scared.

"We're here to apply for a marriage license, please," Herman said.

The woman behind the counter laughed. "Sorry, I can't help you."

"You can't?" my mother asked.

"No, I can't. This is the dog license window."

Mom turned to Herman and said, "It's not too late. If you want to change your mind, we can just walk out."

Herman took her hand, kissed it, and said to the clerk, "Maybe after we're married, we'll come back to you. But can you tell us where to go for our marriage license?"

"Upstairs and to the right," the clerk chuckled.

THE FOLLOWING WEEK Betty and Herman went to pick out their rings. Mom selected a delicate band of graceful diamond and yellow gold leaves. Herman chose a solid gold ring in which they had inscribed the last name Liss, and before it, the initial B for Betty: "BLISS."

HERMAN AND BETTY'S WEDDING at Temple Emanuel in West Hartford, Connecticut was as enchanting as the name inside the golden ring. August 18, 1974 dawned brilliant, and the morning ceremony was aglow with sunlight filtered through stained glass. The wedding was intimate—family and a few close friends. The bride wore a silk peach-colored dress with a matching broad-brimmed hat. Herman, in a charcoal gray suit and peach and gray striped tie, was as dashing as she was exquisite. I, as the matron of honor, and my brother as best man, walked our mother down the aisle. Herman's eyes teared watching his bride approach.

The rabbi blessed Herman and Betty's union. As they stood under the wedding canopy, he spoke of the four pillars of a happy marriage—faith, friendship, love, and kindness. Each of these supports, I knew, were firmly planted. They would only grow.

Following the service, the wedding luncheon was held in a private room at a lakeside restaurant. There were toasts and good wishes, lots of laughter, and love. "*L'Chaim!* To Life!" everyone cheered.

When it was my turn to speak, I said, "Herman, Mom's not the only one in this family who has fallen in love with you. You are a treasure to all of us. If it's all right with you, we would like the privilege of calling you Dad and Grandpa."

Herman, who never had children of his own, was now father to a son and daughter and grandfather to a three-year-old boy. Scott jumped up from the table, ran over to Herman, and leaped into his lap. He nestled into his new grandfather's arms. Our little family felt complete.

Then Herman and Betty toasted each other. Champagne glass in hand, Herman said, "Sweetheart, my deepest wish is that we live to celebrate our twenty-fifth anniversary in good health and happiness."

Mom nodded her head and laughed. "Herman, you'll be ninety, and I'll be eighty."

"God willing!" he beamed.

AUTUMN LOVE

FOLLOWING THE RECEPTION, THE NEWLYWEDS LEFT
for a honeymoon on Cape Cod. They swam in the Atlantic,
sailed in the harbors, danced in the moonlight, and strode
the beaches from Plymouth to Provincetown, hand in hand. Herman
and Betty promised each other that for as long as God willed it, they
would welcome each new possibility.

Herman moved into Betty's apartment and commuted to his job
in New Haven. Mom eagerly resumed her role as administrative assistant in a drug rehabilitation hospital. Each morning Herman rose
before dawn to attend religious services before his lengthy drive. In the
evening, whenever he could, he joined the congregation for services on
his way home. Their days were filled with faith and love and boundless
wonder.

Betty's lifelong dream of "going to the seashore" was nurtured by
Herman's wish to celebrate life with his beloved. And celebrate they
did! Neither of them had traveled far before, but now when Betty's
Connecticut state employees' association offered trips, they were the
first to sign up.

Betty and Herman played in the turquoise waters of Hawaii, Ber-
muda, the Bahamas, and the Caribbean. They watched whales in
Mexico and Alaska. They climbed the steps of the Acropolis in Greece
and reached the summit of Masada in Israel. They rode a camel in
Egypt and a rickshaw in Hong Kong. They explored open-air markets
in the Canary Islands and Morocco. Wherever they went, it was hand
in hand.

Together the couple uncovered the fun and adventure in even the simplest of moments. Laughter was the backbeat of their life. Herman pretended to call McDonald's and ask for a reservation for "the best seat in the house." Invariably he'd follow with, "And oh—we'd like a bottle of your finest champagne!" Betty would laugh and say, "He's such a sport!"

Whenever my family came to visit, on the door would be a new welcome sign designed by Herman. He lovingly decorated it with pictures clipped from greeting cards and magazines. Hand-drawn hearts and arrows framed the posters and his loving words. These same hearts encircled poems he wrote for Mom, sometimes written on napkins and served with the evening snacks he prepared for her.

Even trips to the supermarket were occasions for delicious silliness. Dad, in his element, would scour the aisles looking for kosher items, and I'd be scouting for all-natural food. Mom, who loved to eat but hated shopping, would roll her eyes and say, "You know, this store is open twenty-four hours a day. Why don't the two of you come together at three in the morning, run up and down the aisles reading every label, and really have a good time!" We'd leave the store doubled over.

Herman's special delight was being a grandpa. Whatever Scott's fascination or frustration, his grandfather was there to listen and to understand. For a man who never raised children, Herman intuitively knew both how to hold his grandson close and how to encourage him to fly.

When Scott was a little boy, he and his grandfather would march hand in hand on the beach, belting out the Air Force song "Off We Go Into the Wild Blue Yonder." On summer evenings we'd play family card games, and when Scott grew restless or was losing and would throw in his cards, his grandfather smiled and said, "You can play with us tomorrow night." And he did.

In the mornings when his grandparents visited, Scott would climb into bed with them, and they'd laugh and tickle and make up games. Their favorite was 'Sleeping Princess!' Either Scott or Herman would kiss Betty on the cheek. She'd open her eyes in mock astonishment and the guys would cry out, "Who woke up the sleeping princess?" Betty would then try to guess who kissed her. They'd kiss and guess and giggle some more. This game held its delight for years.

One day when Scott was a young teen, we all went clothes shopping. I saw him whisper something in his grandpa's ear. They came to tell us that they were going to the pharmacy next door. Mom and I finished early and went to look for them. I heard muffled laughter in the back of the store. The two of them were huddled together enjoying the latest issue of *Playboy*.

At seventy Herman was still working, still in love with his job as manager and salesman for an Italian food distributor. The position required driving to stores in Connecticut, Rhode Island, and New Jersey. Late one winter night, after he returned from a five-hour trip on icy roads, Mom met him at the door.

"You can't keep doing this!" she pleaded. "It's too dangerous for you to drive in this weather. And then you're carrying heavy boxes in slippery parking lots. I worry every time you leave the house. I wish you would retire."

"You're still working," he answered. "I wouldn't consider retiring before you do."

Mom had been at the hospital for nearly ten years and delighted in her job and her colleagues. On weekends, young doctors from around the world who trained at the hospital came to visit Betty and Herman, their adopted American parents. She knew she'd miss her work. But if it meant that Herman would be safe, she'd retire.

In the spring, Betty and Herman embarked on their next adventure.

Florida and Cape Cod became their new playgrounds. Herman and Betty purchased a small one-bedroom condominium at King's Point, a retirement community in Delray Beach, where they spent the winters. The rest of the year Mom and Dad lived in our summer home in Yarmouth, Massachusetts.

The opportunity to live near the shore was a source of constant amazement. Each day when they rose, Herman would ask, "Sweetheart, where would you like to go today?" They'd pack a lunch and set out to explore. Together Betty and Herman discovered new beaches and coves and parks, met wonderful new friends, took courses, and attended theater. At sixty and seventy, life was fresh and new.

Each school vacation we'd join my parents in Florida. They shared their little home and enormous hearts. Somehow, we never felt cramped. Every morning we'd awaken to the sound of Dad squeezing fresh orange juice as he and Mom excitedly planned our day.

Over the years our spirited guides escorted us to Disney World, Sea World, Circus World, a polo match, and boat rides on the Everglades. Our favorite trip was our annual pilgrimage to Lion Country Safari, where Dad drove the car through the park while the animals roamed free. The Toyota rocked with laughter as we watched the elephant pick up a beam to smack the rhinoceros on the head. We'd go crazy as the ostrich peered into our windshield or the lion cubs trailed their mother right in front of us. Our joy in these precious days together never dimmed.

On summer mornings we'd head for the Cape Cod beaches and stay until dusk. Mom and Dad played for hours in the water, swimming side by side, floating, or holding one another as the other rested on the waves. In the evening we'd go out for ice cream, return to the beach to admire the sky, or stay home and play cards or Scrabble.

Each night before bed Herman would sing an Italian love song to Betty. After completing his off-key rendition he would ask hopefully, "Encore?" Mom would giggle, shake her head and exclaim, "No!" That never stopped him.

For fifteen years, every autumn and spring Betty and Herman packed their car and traveled between Cape Cod and Florida. They honored their pledge to appreciate each day, each opportunity, and each other.

WHEN BETTY WAS SEVENTY-FIVE, she was diagnosed with diabetes—the disease that took her father and several other family members. She determined that as best she could she would meet this new challenge with courage and optimism.

Mom learned to inject herself and monitor her blood sugar. Her signature humor spilled over even here. She decorated a white wicker basket and filled it with her needles and testing equipment. One early morning during my visit, she donned a red cape over her nightgown and came out carrying her flowered basket festooned with colored ribbons.

"Who are you?" I asked.

"Little Red Riding Hood," came the reply.

Herman had a new mission. He took it upon himself to find every allowable food that would entice Betty.

I noticed that now when he shopped, he searched for labels indicating kosher and sugar-free. When he found one he'd bring it to me and ask, "Do you think Mom would like this?" When I answered "yes," he'd put it in his basket and beam.

Herman, then eighty-five, was beginning to experience his own challenges, though like Betty he didn't complain. He coped with severe arthritic pain in his knees, making it difficult for him to stand or walk a distance. A cane and knee supports provided some relief. Breathlessness followed even mild exertion. Herman was also treated for facial skin cancer and told that it was unlikely to return.

Mom developed searing leg and foot pain due to the diabetes. Herman and Betty, now both unsteady, braced themselves to support each other. Whoever was standing would offer an arm to help the other rise from the bed or chair.

Through love and will, they held each other up.

At eighty-nine, Herman was still driving. Now, though, when they traveled north and south they shipped the car and flew. In November 1998, the morning after arriving in Florida, Herman left Betty sleeping and went out to buy oranges to surprise her with juice for their first breakfast. Turning left at a busy intersection, Herman misjudged the distance and speed of the oncoming car. It struck his passenger side with such force that it slammed him against the steering wheel. The officer at the scene reported that had my mother been in the car, she would have been killed. Herman was hospitalized with cuts, bruises, and abnormal heart rhythm.

Life became increasingly difficult. Herman and Betty were far from home and family and without transportation. That winter most days were spent in bed with Dad recuperating and Mom lying by his side. It was clear that they could no longer continue to travel or to live alone. Their minds were still sharp, their spirits resolute, but their bodies were changing.

I was endlessly concerned for their safety. How relieved I was when during my winter visit Mom told me, "Honey, I don't think we can come back to Florida again. It's much too hard for us to manage."

"You're right," I replied. "Would you and Dad consider moving to a retirement complex closer to our home? The Cape is too far for me to reach you in an emergency, and in the winter you'd be isolated there. If you and Dad agree, I can start looking for a new place where you'd be safe and happy."

After much reflection, Betty and Herman agreed to give up both Florida and Cape Cod. I called and visited countless facilities, but not one was a match. The residents were largely confused, depressed, dependent. I attended sessions given by elder affairs attorneys and community home health agencies. What an education I received—but not an answer that was right for them. My parents were still vital, joyful people with the capacity to learn and grow. They needed stimulation, opportunities to meet astute people, to be a part of a thriving adult community where they could receive the support they required. But where?

Each weekend in the spring I traveled to the Cape to shop for them, do their laundry, clean, and cook. Often I took days off from teaching to take them to their doctors' appointments. Each Sunday evening when I left, my heart sank. How would they manage? Would they be safe until I returned?

Then a miracle happened. I received a call from the Jack Satter House, a model elder housing community in Revere, Massachusetts, right on Revere Beach. A few years earlier we had visited distant relatives there, and my parents, struck by the beauty of the setting and the friendliness of people, placed their names on the waiting list. Because of the uniqueness of the facility, the wait was many years long.

The director of housing called me in May 1999, five years after our visit, to ask, "Are your parents still interested in an apartment at the Satter House? If they are, there will be a one-bedroom unit available in July."

It was an answer to a prayer! The Satter House, a modern, nine-story apartment complex, offered amenities that were ideal for my parents. The residents were vigorous and ran religious services, the coffee shop, their own food store, and the library. Incredibly, it was right across from Revere Beach, just yards from the house where my mother grew up. And as a special bonus for Betty, right next door was Kelly's Famous Roast Beef, a stand that featured fried clams every bit as delicious as those from her childhood.

On July 4th, sixty years after moving away, my Mom returned to her beloved Revere Beach. This time she came back with Herman. She was home.

HERMAN AND BETTY were awestruck. How could this have happened? At their ages they were given an opportunity to begin anew. On their first morning in their sixth floor ocean view apartment, they pulled back the curtains and gasped. The sun danced on the jet blue waves along a wide swath of Revere Beach—the sand and the sea where Betty played as a girl.

Now each afternoon Mom and Dad walked arm and arm across the street to the boardwalk where Betty and her family used to relax on late, hot summer nights. Fingers entwined, they watched the waves, laughed at the gulls drifting on the breeze, and delighted in the children chasing the surf. In the evening they'd sit together in their living room, hand in hand, admiring the moonlight path shining across the sea. "Thank God!" they'd say.

SIX WEEKS AFTER THEIR MOVE to Revere, we had an exuberant celebration of life, of love, of return. On August 18th Herman turned ninety. It was Betty and Herman's twenty-fifth wedding anniversary.

Family and friends gathered to honor this incredible couple. After a seafood dinner at a beachfront restaurant, we returned to the Satter House Community Room, which was decorated with pictures of Betty and Herman in their youth, at their wedding, and on their travels. My friends, "Herman's Girls," presented stories, songs, and dances in honor of the couple who shared such joy with each one of them over the years.

After the entertainment Herman rose to thank us all and to offer his own toast. "Sweetheart, twenty-five years ago, on our wedding day, I made a wish. I wished that God grant us the gift of celebrating this special anniversary. I thank God, and I thank you, for making me the luckiest man alive."

Just as we had a quarter century before, we lifted our glasses and cheered, "*L'Chaim!* To Life!"

PART II

A NEW LIFE

AT EIGHTY AND NINETY, HERMAN AND BETTY EM-braced their new life at the Satter House with boundless en-thusiasm. Lectures, entertainment, and bus trips enlivened their days. Herman became active in the Satter House temple, and Betty marveled at the wonder of again living on Revere Beach.

The morning after the move, Herman and Betty met two of their new hall neighbors. Herman had opened the apartment door to take in his paper, and in strode a handsome orange and white striped cat. The cat looked at him up and down, sat at his feet, and purred.

From outside the door Herman heard, "Whiskers—Whiskers—you can't do that!"

Dad opened the door, "You're welcome to come in, too," he said to the woman who followed the cat.

"I'm sorry about the intrusion," she said. "We just moved in, and my cat ran out of our apartment. He didn't know where to find me. This is Whiskers, and I'm Fran."

Dad introduced himself, called to Mom, and invited Fran and Whiskers to stay for coffee and cream.

"Thank you," Fran said. "But we can't just now. I'm unpacking."

"Can I help you in any way?" Herman asked.

"You already have," Fran laughed. "Whiskers has a new friend. He's usually very shy and runs from strangers and hides. Now if Whiskers disappears, I'll know where to look!"

Fran and Whiskers, Betty and Herman became the best of friends. They were like family. On warm evenings they would sit outside together and share the stories of their lives. As the weather grew cooler they would meet in the lobby, exchange memories, and make plans for the week. Fran was a colorful storyteller, and Betty and Herman were her best audience.

They would laugh heartily at her tales, and Dad would say, "Fran, you could be the entertainment here. You should do a one-woman show."

Whiskers, too, was a part of the team. When my parents came to visit Fran in her apartment, Dad would place his cane on the table. The cat would bat it with its paw, and Herman would knock it back to him. It became their special game.

"You know," Fran confided in me, "when I'm with Betty and Herman, I can share anything. We just have to look at each other, and we understand."

Years younger than my parents, Fran told me that she would often pretend they were her own. "I'm used to sharing them," I told her.

Nearly each afternoon I'd come to visit, and we'd go for rides, to shop, or to doctors' appointments. As we passed Mom's birthplace—just around the corner from their new home—she'd chuckle, "Put your hand over your heart." We always did. She'd share the stories of her youth—stories that I found tiresome and old-fashioned when I was growing up. Suddenly these tales were precious to me. I couldn't get enough. Finally I understood why Revere had such a powerful hold on my mother. The wind, the sand, and the tides captivated me as well.

As SUMMER TURNED to fall, the activity calendar at the Satter house became even fuller. Each holiday was celebrated with a party and entertainment, and Halloween would be the first major event for my parents in their new community. In anticipation of a costume party and prizes, Herman and Betty began their preparations early.

"Sweetheart," Betty said. "How would you feel about going to the Halloween party dressed in a beach theme?" Her eyes danced.

"What are you thinking?" Herman asked.

"Well, I think you'd make a spectacular bathing beauty!"

"Bathing beauty! You mean me, dressed as a woman?"

"Yes," Mom said. "I have a gorgeous hot pink and black bathing suit that I'm sure would fit you. Michele, could you find Dad a wig? We could decorate your cane to match your outfit."

Herman's face lit up, "Well, I suppose we could stuff the top of the suit with my socks."

I found a long, curly blonde wig. Shopping for that wig, I saw young mothers looking for costumes for their children. I bet I was the only one there looking for flaxen hair for her ninety-year-old father!

Dad had fuschia and black knee braces that perfectly coordinated with the bathing suit. I decorated the cane with matching crepe paper that wound around the base and fluttered at the top. Herman stuffed the cups of Mom's suit with two pairs of socks. Across his chest, from his left shoulder to his right hip, he wore a white sash with the words "Miss *Sadder* House." Mom applied bright blue eye shadow, midnight mascara, and cherry lipstick. The stunning bathing beauty sported a trim white mustache.

As Herman marched into the dining room in the Halloween procession of ten contestants, he positioned himself at the end of the line. When he entered the hall, one hundred and fifty people roared. They cheered and hooted and hollered. Light bulbs flashed. Herman won first prize.

HALLOWEEN, HANUKKAH, Christmas, New Year's Eve, Valentine's Day, Easter, Passover, the Fourth of July— the first year at the Satter House was one of celebration of each holiday, each day.

Although by the spring both of my parents were using walkers, it was just their bodies that had slowed, not their hearts or their minds.

IN AUGUST 2000, Mom began to fall. She cried out in pain when rising from a chair, and one day the walker could no longer support her. The diabetic neuropathy in her knees became so extreme that she could bear no weight. Stabbing sensations shot through her legs from hips to ankles, and one morning when trying to stand she crumpled to the floor. Betty was rushed to the emergency room by ambulance and admitted for an evaluation.

My mother's pain was intractable. She was unable to move, even in bed. Her height and her size necessitated that four nurses lift her on a sheet toward the head of the bed each time she slid down toward the foot. The doctors prescribed a series of painkillers, but nothing brought relief. After two weeks, they placed her on the powerful drug OxyContin.

The doctors didn't know if Betty would ever be able to walk again or perform the simplest of tasks for herself. They insisted that only at a rehabilitation center would there be any possibility of improvement—but they gave us little hope.

Herman, now living at the Satter House alone, was separated from Betty for the first time in twenty-six years. He missed her desperately, and each day sat by her side for hours, holding her hand through the bars that kept her from falling out of bed. In the early morning, before I picked him up, he went to the synagogue to pray for her recovery. When asked "How's Betty?" he would reply, "God is good. We believe in miracles, and I know she's coming home."

Every day he told me, "Don't give up hope. You know that Mom's favorite expression is 'Money lost is nothing lost. Hope lost is everything lost.' In our minds we have to see her walking into our little apartment, coming home to us. It will happen. You'll see!"

Mom was transferred to the rehabilitation center, again by ambulance. On admittance the doctor asked her, as she lay motionless on the bed, "What are your goals, Mrs. Liss?"

She shot back, "To walk and to get the hell out of here!"

Mom's humor and feistiness charmed the therapists. They worked with her during scheduled sessions and would visit her during their breaks. Over the weeks, the physical and occupational therapists shared their hopes and dreams with Betty as they were working to help her achieve her own. Each time she made the slightest gain, there were whoops of joy.

As the OxyContin became effective, initial strengthening was done on the bed. They taught Betty to rebuild her muscles by drawing the alphabet with her feet. Herman, sitting in the chair next to her, did the same. Within three weeks increases in the medication allowed Mom to stand, at first for moments and then for minutes. In time, Betty began to walk.

Herman was his wife's greatest cheerleader. They would practice walking together, each haltingly pushing a walker and stopping every few feet to rest. A therapist would follow them with a wheelchair should either need to sit.

Herman would call out, "Good job, sweetheart. Keep it up and we'll be dancing soon. I need you to design my Halloween costume this year. Halloween is in only two more months. You'll be home before then. You'll see!"

Each evening when it was time for me to take Dad back to the Satter House, he would kiss the top of Mom's head and say, "Little baby, sleep well, and I'll be here tomorrow." Then he would sing his Italian love song, still off key, and ask hopefully, "Encore?"

Mom's answer, with a giggle, was still "NO!"

FIVE WEEKS AFTER she was admitted to the rehabilitation center, Betty returned home. She refused to be wheeled into the building. "I can walk!"

With me by her side, we rode up in the elevator and slowly made our way to the front door of the apartment. It was covered in colorful signs that read "I Love You Sweetheart" and "Welcome Home" and "Believe in Miracles." We knocked and Dad opened the door. Betty and Herman embraced, tears running down their cheeks.

Mom received support in the morning from aides who bathed her and helped her dress. Therapists came to their home to continue the strengthening and balance exercises. Each afternoon I was there to take them to doctors, or shop, go for rides, play Scrabble, talk, and put their medicine together. I had just retired after thirty years as a special educator teaching children with physical, cognitive, social, behavioral, and emotional challenges. Now I was able to devote myself to taking care of my parents, just as my mother had done for my grandmother during five years of treatment for colon cancer. It seemed natural that I would do the same. I remembered my mother's devotion to her mother, as well as her exhaustion, worry, and frustration throughout my grandmother's suffering. I thought I was prepared, but was to learn that the anguish and the love of the caregiver were both beyond measure.

My admiration for Herman only grew. His patience knew no bounds. The OxyContin reduced Mom's frustration tolerance, and even the slightest, unintentional provocation could disturb her. Dad often inadvertently bumped the furniture with his heavyweight, extra large four-wheeled walker. Mom would get upset. Each time she chastised him, he'd look at her and say, "I'm sorry, sweetheart. I'll try not

73

to do it again."

Sometimes within minutes the walker would hit the table or sofa or even her chair leg, and the scene would be repeated. Mom's annoyance would increase, but Dad remained calm and understanding.

He'd prepare special snacks, and tried in every way to relieve her. At night when Mom woke up with cramps or shooting pains in her feet and legs, Herman would get out of bed and do a massage. His anguish on seeing her suffer was as great as the physical pain Betty endured. Each time there was distress in her voice or in her eyes, I would see Dad wince.

Still, they laughed together. Halloween was coming, and Betty and Herman planned his costume. This year he was to be a hula dancer. One of the visiting nurses loaned Dad a grass skirt made with green plastic strips. It didn't quite fit around his waist, so I extended it with pieces cut from a heavy-duty leaf bag. Herman wore Mom's turquoise silk bra, again stuffed with his sports socks. A scarlet blossom tucked behind his right ear punctuated a long, straight black wig. Tropical fabric flowers festooned the walker. Around Herman's neck was a Hawaiian lei. Fran and Whiskers came to watch as Mom and I transformed this ninety-one year old, six-foot-tall gentleman into an island beauty. Fran was our makeup consultant. Again, Herman won first prize!

TRANSITIONS

BETWEEN THE **H**ALLOWEEN **H**ULA OF 2000 AND Dad's more modest angel incarnation the following year, there were profound changes and challenges for both Betty and Herman. Dad's breathlessness increased, and at ninety-two he was diagnosed with congestive heart failure. Herman's energy declined, and bed became his respite. Sleep provided relief from both his arthritic pain and irregular breathing.

At the same time, Mom's diabetes flared. She required ever more stringent pain management to control the piercing sensations in her hands, feet, and legs. Unlike Dad, sleep did not come easily to her. Increasing doses of pain medication evoked more powerful side effects. Both her appetite and patience suffered.

In spite of their struggles, each late afternoon they'd get dressed and prepare for dinner in the community dining room. Mom carefully selected her earrings, necklace, and bracelets to coordinate with her outfit. Her makeup complemented the color scheme. From the hall closet Dad would call, "Sweetheart, does this shirt match these pants?" He'd drape the shirt over his walker and bring it into the bedroom for Mom's approval.

At five o'clock, as Herman and Betty waited to enter the dining hall, their friend and housing director, Barbara Assa, would ask, "How are you tonight?"

"Truthfully, I'm still in pain," Betty would say. "But I put on my lipstick, and I come down to see you and my friends, and I know I am alive!"

Barbara later told me, "Their humor and their love carried them through. Herman and Betty were an inspiration to all of us. They were the epitome of what growing old together should be. Even when they were ill, it was obvious how much in love they were. There are so few people who have that kind of total commitment, complete connection. They were like one. They were inseparable. They got it right!"

ON THE EVENING of January 31, 2002, there was a fierce ice storm. My phone rang at 9:30. It was Dad. "Michele, something's wrong with Mom. She's lying on the bed, but one leg is hanging down to the floor. Her eyes are closed, and she's mumbling. I can't understand her."

"Dad, call 911 immediately. We'll meet you at the hospital!"

When the ambulance arrived, Herman asked to ride with Betty. They took Mom on a stretcher and Dad in a wheelchair. There was no time for him to walk. The driver let Herman sit up front, next to him.

In spite of the treacherous roads Betty was taken not to the closest hospital, but to Massachusetts General Hospital, where there would be neurologists ready to evaluate and treat her. By the time my husband and I arrived in Boston she had already had a CAT scan.

Mom had had a stroke, a bleed to the brain. It would be a few days before they knew the extent of the damage.

Dad sat slumped in the chair next to Mom's bed, caressing her with his eyes. "Maybe there was something I could have done, should have done, so this wouldn't have happened. I didn't know what was wrong. She didn't answer me. She just laid there," he cried.

"Dad, you couldn't have prevented this. You did everything right."

He just shook his head. The beep of the heart monitor and the whir of the oxygen played against the rhythm of the sleet on the window.

"We're going to take you home now, Dad," said my husband, David.

"No, I don't want to leave Mom. I'll sleep in the chair. I'll be OK."

"Dad, please, you have to come with us. You need to take your medicine. You have to rest. I promise we'll come back early," I pleaded.

Reluctantly, Dad allowed us to wheel him to the car. It was 3 a.m.

At 8:00 in the morning Herman was ready to go back to the hospital.

"Dad, you have to sleep and you need a good breakfast. Anyway,

Mom will be having tests this morning."

"Can we get there in time to help her with her lunch?" Dad gently urged.

We entered Mom's room at noon. She had just returned from a series of tests and smiled weakly when she saw us. The doctor came in and said, "Mrs. Liss, I'm going to ask you a few questions, if it's OK?"

He asked a series of orientation questions. "Do you know where you are? What day is it? Who is the president?"

Mom didn't respond.

Then he said, "Mrs. Liss, can you count for me?"

She obliged. *"Ain, tzvay, drie, feer—"* Mom was counting in Yiddish.

"How are you feeling, Mrs. Liss?"

"Mine caup teet mer vay." My head hurts.

I signaled the doctor to meet me outside the room. "What's going on?" I asked. "Why isn't my mother speaking English?"

"That sometimes happens after a stroke. People sometimes revert to their first language."

"But my mother's first language was English!"

"Did she learn Yiddish as a young child?"

"Yes, she learned it in her home."

"Well, that's it. It's the language that brings her comfort. That's how the brain works. Her roommate only answers now in Italian."

"Oh, my God. Will my mother ever return?"

"We'll know in a few days how extensive the damage is. I know this is very hard for all of you."

By the next day Mom was speaking English, although somewhat haltingly. Her sentences were short and her vocabulary was sparse. She struggled to remember names. Her humor though, was still intact.

"They keep asking me 'Where are you?' What do they care? I never knew where I was before! Why should I know now?" Mom was right. She had the worst sense of direction of anyone I'd ever met.

What she *did* know was that wherever she was that morning, she did not want to be there. She wanted to be home. Needless to say, that's what Herman wanted as well. After two weeks and numerous tests, the doctors agreed to allow her to return to the Satter House with the support of visiting nurses, therapists, and aides. I would spend the nights until she grew stronger.

I slept on the sofa in the living room that first night. At 6:00 a.m. I was awakened by a crash. Racing into the bedroom, I saw that Mom had fallen backwards on a chair, her head against the wall and her feet in the air. She was limp and unable to speak.

"Please send an ambulance to the Satter House. Sixth floor, apartment 624. I think my mother just had another stroke."

The ambulance came within minutes. Mom was strapped onto a stretcher and taken back to Mass General Hospital. Dad and I followed in my car.

To our relief, Mom did not have another stroke. She had acquired a urinary tract infection in the hospital from the catheter. Urinary tract infections can temporarily mimic stroke symptoms in older people, affecting speech, reasoning, and coordination.

Huge doses of antibiotics cleared the infection, but this time we all agreed that Mom needed some time in a skilled nursing center to monitor her health and build her strength.

A FEW DAYS LATER Betty was transferred to a rehabilitation center on the North Shore of Boston, close to Revere. There she received speech, physical, and occupational therapy.

Dad and I joined Mom every afternoon. Rather than return to bed and rest after lunch as he had before Mom's stroke, Dad was usually dressed and ready to visit when I arrived to make his noon meal. His strength and energy seemed to rebound. He willed himself to help her recover and return home. They walked together in the hall. When the center had live entertainment they'd sit side by side and sing along. Dad brought pictures of their trips to help Mom remember their sweetest days.

"One day we'll travel again, sweetheart. You'll see," he'd say to her. "Where do you want to go?"

"To Alaska or Greece. Even to New York," Mom answered.

"When you're well, we'll go wherever you like!"

AFTER TWO WEEKS Betty was to be discharged, and I scheduled a doctor's appointment for the day before her return home. When I arrived to pick Mom up for her examination, I found her sitting in the oversized hospital chair near the window.

"Hi, beautiful. We're going to see Dr. Graham today."

She didn't respond. Her eyes were glassy. I felt her forehead. She was burning. I ran to the nurses' station. "Something is wrong with my mother. She's not talking. She's sick!"

The nurse raced to her room. "Betty, are you OK?"

Mom shook her head.

He took her temperature. It was 103. The nurse pointed to me. "Do you know who this is?"

Mom nodded, but didn't answer.

"How old is she?"

"Twelve."

Tears burned my eyes. I couldn't believe it. How much more could she endure? This was an endless nightmare, and we weren't waking up.

The nurse wheeled Mom to my car and helped to lift her in. She was limp when I draped the seat belt around her. We drove to the doctor, but I could barely see through my tears. I kept talking to Mom, trying to reassure her and myself that we'd get help. I parked, ran up the flight of stairs, and asked for someone to bring down a wheelchair to push my mother up the steep ramp. A slight male nurse came to our aid. He lifted Betty, much taller and heavier than he, into the chair. Together we wheeled her into the building.

The doctor saw her immediately. "I'm not certain what's wrong, Michele. She has to go to the hospital. Now!"

For the third time in a month Betty was taken by ambulance to Massachusetts General Hospital. There she was diagnosed with Influenza A, a virulent form of the flu. Mom was put into quarantine. Herman was not allowed to visit her because of his age and susceptibility. Only the staff and I could enter her room, protected by a mask, gown, and gloves.

Each day after leaving my mother, I'd drive to Dad's apartment and check on him.

"How's Mom? Is she better today?"

I'd share any shred of hope, searching for even the slightest glimmer.

"Did she ask for me?" he'd wonder.

"Yes," I always replied. But she hadn't.

"You'll see," he'd respond. "Mom will be well. She'll come home."

I wasn't so sure.

Two more weeks in Mass General Hospital and the infection had cleared. Still, Betty had lost strength. The effect of the stroke, the urinary tract infection, and the flu left her physically and emotionally drained. Mom was transferred to yet another rehabilitation center. This one, Shaughnessy-Kaplan, was attached to Salem Hospital.

"We're so lucky that Mom's being admitted here," Dad told me. "You know, everyone at the Satter House says that it's one of the best rehabs in New England. With God's help, Mom will get well here. We mustn't lose hope."

Where did Herman get his strength? He was ninety-two and himself ill, but, you'd never know it. He wouldn't stay home and rest, not even for a day. It was exhausting for him to walk, and I wanted to wheel him down the long hall to Mom's room, but he refused.

"No," he'd say. "It's important for Mom to see me walk. I don't want her to worry about me."

As the days progressed, Betty's stamina and balance improved. Yet the combined effects of illness and medication were obvious. Her natural spontaneity and humor were clouded by pain.

One afternoon Betty asked Herman to change the TV channel. Never technologically facile, the new remote baffled Dad. As he puzzled over the multiple buttons, Mom snapped, "What's taking you so long? Anyone could figure it out!"

I showed Dad what to do and then had to leave the room. My eyes were stinging. I needed to get away. It destroyed me to hear her speak to him like that. I knew it was the medicine talking, but still it hurt. Dad, though, never challenged her, never pushed back. His love and devotion were boundless.

As I walked the halls, it hit me. It's easy to love when there's health and good fortune. What's not so easy, really God-like, is to stay in the love when your heart is breaking.

In mid-March, six weeks and five admissions after Betty became ill, she returned home. Herman patiently, lovingly cared for her with the assistance of nurses, aides, therapists, and myself. He sat by her side, held her hand, and caressed her hair, asking gently, "Sweetheart, is there anything I can do for you?"

When Betty was unable to get out of bed, Herman brought her drinks and the snacks she favored, carrying them on the tray of his walker. He still clipped coupons, made his grocery lists, and when able came with me to the store to hunt for new, tempting foods for Mom.

Mostly, though, they both slept—although to Dad's sorrow they could no longer sleep together. Even the slightest touch to Betty's feet or legs made her cringe. Their own bed was replaced by two hospital beds, one to relieve Herman's labored breathing, the other to keep Betty from falling to the floor.

DEVOTION

"I CAN'T WAKE MY WIFE! PLEASE, SEND AN AMBU-
lance. I think she's had a stroke!"

On Sunday morning, August 4, 2002—fifteen weeks
after Betty's return—Herman found her in bed, unresponsive, breathing shallowly, her mouth twisted to one side.

This time the stroke was massive. Although Mom regained consciousness, she barely spoke and was unable to walk or feed herself.
Two weeks in the hospital and five weeks at Shaughnessy-Kaplan Rehabilitation Center produced no gains. Mom only grew weaker.

Herman steadfastly remained by her side, willing her to live, willing
himself to be strong.

Each morning I'd arrive at the Satter House to make Dad's breakfast
and help him dress. We'd reach Mom's in time for lunch, and Herman
insisted on feeding her himself. Betty could no longer get the spoon to
her mouth, and the aides fed her when we were not there. The doctor
prescribed a special diet designed to prevent her from choking. While
feeding Betty, Herman balanced himself against the bed's railing so he
wouldn't fall. "Sweetheart, it's time to eat. Please open your mouth."
Dad dipped the spoon into her bowl and gingerly placed the food on
her tongue. "Remember to chew—chew some more, sweetheart—
swallow now."

After a few mouthfuls Mom would fall back to sleep. Dad would
wipe her mouth, kiss her forehead, and settle back in the chair, never
taking his eyes off his Sleeping Princess.

HERMAN'S NINETY-THIRD BIRTHDAY and Betty and Herman's twenty-eighth anniversary came two weeks after her stroke. How do you celebrate in the midst of anguish? Yet how do you not? My family gathered in Mom's room with cake, ice cream, balloons, and presents.

"Mom," I said. "Today is a special day. It's your anniversary and Dad's birthday."

Then I named everyone there. "Dad is here, and your son, Barry, and your grandchildren, Scott and Cindy, and your son-in-law, David, and me."

Mom smiled weakly and gazed toward the window. She reached out her hand and whispered the only word she said that day. "Ma?"

"No," I said. "Grandma's not here, but I know she's watching over us."

Since this latest stroke my mother would, on occasion, raise her eyes, look to the right, and call her mother's name.

Scott took me aside. "Mom," he said to me, "we don't know. Maybe Grandma's mother is here with her. Maybe Grandma can see what we can't!"

Dad offered his traditional birthday-anniversary toast, this time over ginger ale.

"Remember sweetheart, you are my queen. God is good. He loves you. Everyone loves you. Everyone wants you to be well. Please get strong and come back to our little home."

Mom didn't respond. She closed her eyes. She was getting ready to leave us. Dad was not ready to let her go.

THE DAY AFTER our gathering I asked the hospital social worker, Jennifer, to meet with Herman and myself to help prepare him for her passing. The gentle support I was trying to provide wasn't working— for either of us.

We met in Jennifer's office. Herman was clearly uncomfortable. Although respectful as always, his body language signaled that he didn't want to be there.

"Mr. Liss, I'm so sorry. I know this is unimaginably hard for you. Mrs. Liss is not getting better. We're not able to help her here at the Rehab. She will have to go to another facility, and we encourage you to think about hospice support for her."

"Hospice! That means that there's no hope. That means giving up! I'm not giving up!" he declared. "God has helped us before. Each time Betty's been sick, she's recovered. We believe in miracles!"

I sat in that office, put my head down, and cried.

A FEW DAYS LATER I was to meet with the hospice nurse to prepare for Mom's move to the nursing home. Before that meeting, though, I had an appointment scheduled for myself, which meant Herman and I would have to miss Betty's lunch.

"It's OK," my father told me. "I'll take the Elder Services van. I want to be there on time." He was so determined that I didn't try to dissuade him.

Just as I had always done, I arrived in Revere that morning to help Dad dress and make his breakfast. "Why don't I go downstairs with you and walk you to the van?" I suggested.

"No, don't worry. I've seen lots of people take the van. They come to the front door," he said.

I didn't want to take away his dignity, so I agreed. "OK, I'll see you later this afternoon and bring you home. Tell Mom I love her."

I planned to remain in the apartment to straighten up until it was time for my appointment. The phone rang. "Michele, thank God you're there!" I recognized the Satter House receptionist's voice. "Your father fell in the parking lot. He's bleeding. We just called the ambulance."

I grabbed some towels, raced down the six flights of stairs, and ran into the parking lot. There lay my father, blood streaming from the side of his face, near his eye. I knelt down next to him. As I applied pressure, he cried, "Don't let them take me to the hospital. I'm all right. I have to see Mom. Please!"

The van driver tried to explain. "Your father saw the van in the lot. I couldn't park near the door because the mail truck was blocking it. I was waiting for it to move. Your father came out into the lot to meet me. He was rushing, tripped, and fell."

I heard the ambulance blaring. The paramedics jumped out, looked at Dad and said, "We're taking you to the emergency room, Mr. Liss."

"No, I can't go. My wife is in the hospital. She needs me."

"Where is she?" the driver asked.

"Salem Hospital," I responded.

"OK, that's where we'll go."

As my father lay in the emergency room, he told the doctors, "My wife is sick. Please let me go! I'm fine."

"Mr. Liss, now we need to take care of you. We have to stitch you up, send you for a scan, and observe you for a while to make certain you're all right. As soon as we discharge you your daughter can wheel you next door to visit your wife."

"Go see Mom," Dad urged. "Don't worry about me. Go, she needs you!"

I spent the next four hours running between buildings so I could be with them both—with my mother who was barely conscious, and with my father who was conscious only of her.

Late that afternoon I met with the hospice nurse in the emergency room. I was making plans for my mother's passing as my father was being wheeled in for a CAT scan. It felt unreal.

Herman was released at dusk. I wheeled him up to Mom's room, and all the way there he questioned. How was she feeling? Was she any better? Was she worried that he wasn't there?

How could I tell him that she never asked?

DAYS LATER, in early October, Betty was transferred to the nursing home for hospice care. Herman, grateful for the compassion and attention of the hospice staff, still couldn't believe that his wife would not survive. Hospice provided support for all of us. The nurses and social worker understood my concern about my father's staunch denial. Could his insistence on her recovery be holding Mom back?

The following Wednesday, during a family meeting, the nurse said to both of us, "I think that Betty may leave us within a few days."

"But she's gotten well before," protested Dad. "We can't give up. We believe in miracles."

"Sometimes, Herman," the nurse gently said, "the miracle is different from our heart's desire."

Herman sat with Betty the rest of that afternoon, all of the next day, and the next. He held her hand and stroked her hair and prayed.

Friday night, October 11, 2002, soon after returning home, the phone rang. My mother had passed away.

Herman put his head in his hands and wept. He cried all night.

ON THE NEXT DAY, the Sabbath, our little family sat in the apartment, staring at the ocean—at each other—at the sky. There and not there.

My brother and I talked about the funeral, both deciding to write a eulogy for our mother. We'd ask Hedy, my dear friend and Mom's "adopted" daughter, to speak as well.

Herman was resting in bed, and we went to tell him our thoughts. He whispered, "And I'll speak, too."

Barry and I looked at each other. How, we wondered, could this ninety-three-year-old man, devastated by his loss, get up to speak at his wife's funeral? Would it be safe for him? Could his heart endure it?

"Maybe, Dad," I suggested, "if you like, you could write something and your grandson, Scott, could read it. It might be easier for you that way."

"No," Herman insisted. "I have to do this myself."

On Sunday we spoke to the rabbi by phone to plan the service. When he asked who would deliver the eulogies, we told him that Hedy, Barry, and I were composing them and that our father wanted to speak as well.

"I don't think that's a good idea," responded the rabbi. "The stress will be enormous, and given your father's age and physical condition, it could be dangerous for him. Please tell Herman that I'd be happy to read whatever he writes, and I'll say that these are his words about Betty."

"We already offered to do that, but he refused. Maybe you should speak to him yourself and see if *you* can convince him."

"Yes, please put him on the phone. I'm sure we can work this out."

"Dad, Rabbi Mintz would like to speak with you." Barry and I listened in on the extensions.

"Herman, I am so sorry for your loss. Betty was a remarkable woman."

"Thank you, Rabbi. May she rest in peace."

"Your children tell me that you would like to write a eulogy. Herman, may I deliver it for you? Speaking at a funeral is very emotional, and I'm concerned for your health."

"Rabbi, please don't worry about me. I'll be all right."

"Just promise me one thing, Herman. Please think about it tonight.

Public speaking under these circumstances can be overwhelming, and I know that your blood pressure is already high. Can we talk tomorrow?"

"Rabbi, thank you. I will consider this tonight and let you know my decision in the morning."

"Rest well, Herman."

"Dad," I said as Herman prepared for bed, "Barry and I think the rabbi is right. Tuesday is going to be very hard for all of us. Please let someone else read your words."

"I will think about it, and we'll talk tomorrow."

Early the next day Herman requested that we call the rabbi.

"Rabbi, I've made my decision. I am going to speak at my wife's funeral. Betty deserves my respect."

HERMAN, SUPPORTED on either side by David and Scott, said in a clear, strong voice, "Betty was a powerful, loving person. God, in His infinite judgment, decreed that she join him. She leaves a heritage of love and kindness. May God rest her soul and grant her everlasting peace. I will love and respect her memory forever."

Soulmates

THE FLAME OF MY MOTHER'S SEVEN-DAY MEMORIAL candle began to flicker out against the molten wax. Herman had placed Betty's picture beside the candle on the dining room table, draping the frame with Mom's good luck red ribbon.

When I arrived at noon my father was still in bed. "Did Dad get up for breakfast?" I asked my brother, who was packing to return home.

"No," Barry said. "He slept all morning. Must be exhausted. I didn't want to wake him."

"Hi, Dad," I called from the bedroom doorway. "Time to wake up. Let's go for a ride. You've been in for a week, and Mom would want us to go out on this beautiful day. I'll make lunch, and we'll drive along the beach, OK?"

No response. Shadows fell across his cheeks.

"Dad, please, wake up," I urged as I bent down to kiss him.

My vision adjusted to the darkened room, and I saw what my heart couldn't see. Dad's eyes were swollen shut. His mouth drooped to the right. Gently I shook him. "Dad, can you hear me?"

Herman's lids fluttered to reveal narrow slits. He made a few guttural sounds.

"Dad, can you sit up?" I asked, my throat closing. "Barry and I will help you."

My brother and I tried to lift him, but he fell back against the pillows.

"Barry, call 911! Dad's had a stroke!"

THE EMTS were by Herman's side in minutes. "Mr. Liss, we need to take you to the hospital. You have to be examined."

Herman shook his head—no.

"Dad, Barry and I will be there with you, I promise."

Herman was strapped to the stretcher, and my brother and I followed them out. As we passed the memorial candle, a black smoke curl rose from the wick.

ONCE AGAIN I was following an ambulance, my heart pierced by a siren's blare. When we arrived, my father, pale and dazed, lay hooked up to monitors and oxygen.

"He's going to have a CAT scan," the doctor explained. "Then we'll admit him for observation."

"Home, please," my father stammered.

"Mr. Liss, we have to figure out what happened. Then we can help you."

He was wheeled away for tests as I remained in the cubicle, filling out paperwork that I could barely see—name, date of birth, marital status—

Just ten days earlier Herman was sitting at Betty's bedside, holding her hand, singing to her, praying for her. Now I was praying for him.

Early the next morning I received a call from the neurologist. "Your father has had a stroke to the back of the brain. Speech and balance have been affected. He's seeing double. We'll have to keep him here for a few days until he's stabilized. His blood pressure is still very high and the heartbeat is irregular. Memory has been affected, likely due to vascular constriction—limited blood flow to the brain. Herman appears to have had small strokes in the past. And what's that on his nose?"

I explained that his facial cancer had returned, but because my mother was so ill my father refused to leave her to go for surgery and the reconstruction that would follow.

"You know," responded the doctor. "He's ninety-three, and we can't predict the extent of this stroke. Some of the symptoms may resolve or they may worsen. We'll have to wait."

When I arrived at the hospital the speech therapist had just evaluated him. She looked concerned. "Your father couldn't remember your mother's name."

Couldn't remember her name? After twenty-eight years he couldn't remember her name! I didn't want to hear this.

"My mother died just a week ago. He only called her 'sweetheart.'" I was clutching, desperate, denying the reality.

"Oh, I'm so sorry! How are you doing?" the therapist asked.

Why did she ask me that? I didn't know. I was numb.

FIVE DAYS LATER Herman was transferred next door to the Shaughnessy-Kaplan Rehabilitation Center, the hospital where Betty's life ebbed. It was so eerily familiar—the therapists, the social worker, the psychologist, the sounds, the odors. It was all the same, yet now it was Dad lying against the white sheets.

Herman didn't talk about his stroke, his condition, his pain. No, he worried about Betty.

"What if Mom's still suffering?" he asked repeatedly. "What if she still is having trouble breathing? What if she still can't walk? What if her mouth is twisted like it was and she can't eat or talk?"

Here was Herman, breathless, unable to stand, in severe pain, garbling his words, yet he was agonizing not about himself, but his dead wife. His anguish was all-consuming, and my reassurance brokered no relief.

I struggled to find the words to comfort, to convince him that Mom was at peace.

"But how do we know for sure?" he choked.

Someone beside his daughter had to still this trembling. I pleaded for help with the social worker, the woman Dad fled from just weeks before as Mom lay dying. "Jennifer, my father is trapped in a nightmare. He keeps reliving my mother's death and fears for her. I can't get through to him."

"I remember how much Herman loved Betty, how devoted he was, how protective," she responded. "He still wants to protect her. I know that your father is a very religious man. What is his belief about what follows death?"

"I don't know. He's never discussed it with me, but he's petrified. It's all he thinks about. It's beyond grief. It's torture."

"May I call the chaplain to meet with him?"

"Yes, please."

That afternoon there was a gentle tap on the open door.

"Mr. Liss, may I come in? I'm Jane Korins, the hospital chaplain."

My father turned to me and I welcomed our visitor.

In floated a presence of light. This vision with an amber halo, gentle eyes, and velvet voice tenderly smiled and took my father's hand in both of hers. For the first time in weeks Herman's brow unfurled.

"Mr. Liss, I'm deeply sorry about your illness and your wife's passing."

"Thank you," Dad responded, welling up. "Would you like to sit down?"

"Yes, I would."

Jane sat by his bed, never taking her eyes from him, still holding his hand. "Mr. Liss. I know that you are a man of faith. Would you like to pray together?"

"I don't have my prayer book," Herman said.

"That's all right. We can pray together in Hebrew, if you like. I have a prayer book with me," Jane said.

Dad looked at her. "Are you Jewish?" he asked quizzically.

"No, but I've studied Judaism and Hebrew, have Jewish patients, and I work with the rabbis on the North Shore."

"Thank you, thank you," Dad responded, placing his other hand over hers.

We prayed together and then sat in silence. This was my chance to speak.

"Dad, please, let's talk with the chaplain about your concerns about Mom. Maybe she can help us find the answer."

Herman bit his lip and quivered. He slowly shook his head. "My wife, may she rest in peace—"

He couldn't go on.

I spoke for him. "Chaplain, my father is worried that my mother is still suffering, that her body is crippled, that she is still in pain."

Jane acknowledged Dad's fears.

"You love your wife and you're worried that her illness is still with her. Is that right?"

Dad's tears flowed, and Jane and I wept with him.

"Herman—may I call you that? What do you believe happens to a person when they die?"

"I don't know," he responded, dropping his gaze. "I didn't think she'd die—not before me. I was so much older. We believed in miracles. I never thought I'd lose her."

"Herman, tomorrow when I come I'd like to bring a tape for you, if you agree. It's by Rabbi Harold Kushner, the author of *When Bad Things Happen to Good People*. Rabbi Kushner lost his young son, so he understands deeply, intimately, about loss and grief and pain. May I bring you the tape?"

"Yes, please," Dad said.

EACH AFTERNOON the chaplain came to sit with Herman, to open a dialogue about death. They spoke of the anguish of the survivor and the possibility that death may open the door to the end of suffering for the one who has passed. Chaplin Korins gently suggested that perhaps now the soul, free of encumbrance, truly lives.

My father would listen thoughtfully, and then when Jane left he would say to me, "No one knows for sure. No one has come back to report."

One evening as Jane and I left the hospital together, I asked, "What can I do to help him? His grief is more debilitating than his stroke."

"While your mother was alive, Herman stayed strong for her. The stroke may have been a reaction to his loss. Your parents were deeply in love—true soul mates—and that is very, very rare. The agony for him is intensely spiritual."

"I thought my father's faith would comfort him, but it hasn't. He doesn't even want me to bring his prayer book. At home he prayed from it each morning and night."

"He's wrestling with God right now. I can feel his love and his struggle. Nothing he believed is working for him. The miracle he expected, prayed for, didn't happen. One day his faith will be a solace again, but right now he's raw and confused. Let him lead you in finding the answers."

I BEGAN TO PRAY more fervently than I ever had before. I prayed for the strength and wisdom to support my father. I prayed for myself.

Each day, with more urgency, Herman asked me, "When can I go home?"

"Dad, maybe we should consider a home where you'll be able to receive the help you need whenever you need it. You won't have to worry about getting your meals or showering, taking your medication at the right time, or being alone. Even though David and I would visit you every day at the Satter House, I don't think you'd be safe living alone."

"I want to go home!" he said. "Mom would want that."

"Why do you think so, Dad?"

"Mom always said that her parents brought her back to Revere to live out her years. She was so happy there as a child, and we were so happy in our little home. Mom loved it there."

Herman believed, I am certain, that only by returning to their apartment could he honor Mom's memory. The furniture, the pictures, even the ocean evoked Betty's spirit. Dad had lost his love and his health all in one week—how could I insist that he give up his home? I vowed that somehow I'd find a way to make it work.

Herman persevered in his work with the therapists. He wanted to learn to walk again, feed and dress himself, and speak more clearly so he could return to the Satter House. Over the weeks, as he grew a little stronger, I arranged for nurses and aides to assist him when he moved back home. I planned to be there each afternoon and evening. Still, I was worried and exhausted.

The day before his discharge Herman rose from bed, grabbed for his walker, and fell. Nurses heard the crash and came running. It took several people to lift him.

"What happened, Herman?" asked a nurse when they got him back into bed.

"I don't know. My toe hurts. I couldn't stand."

The nurse removed his sock and saw the toe, angry and red. They took blood.

Herman had developed gout for the first time in his life. Treatment began immediately, but it would delay his release.

Now I knew without a doubt that he couldn't return safely home. No matter how much assistance I put into place, it wouldn't be enough. Herman needed round-the-clock care and a team of medical people available on site.

I asked to meet with his doctor and explained my concerns about Herman's return home. He agreed that my father's condition was complicated and tenuous, and that a nursing facility was the kindest and safest answer at this time. Now the challenge was to convince Herman.

Rather than face this alone, I requested that the physician, nurses, therapists, social worker, and chaplain meet with Herman and myself to support this move. Dad's relationship with Jane, the chaplain, had grown loving and strong. He called her "my angel." I asked Jane to lead the meeting. Dad was in bed, and I sat on the chair next to him when the group arrived.

"Hi, Herman," smiled Jane as they entered the room. "We're here to talk to you and Michele about your release from the hospital. We want you to know that we're all concerned about your return home. We believe it would be unsafe for you there, and you couldn't receive the care that you need."

Dad's eyes misted. "But I have to go home," he said. "It's what my wife would want."

"Herman, we're concerned about you and believe you'll be safer and happier in a nursing home."

Tears ran down Dad's cheeks. He shook his head no.

This was not going the way I had hoped. I knew I had to be direct. This very moment, with the entire team surrounding his bed, was my best opportunity.

"Dad, the staff and I are worried about your safety. You know, there was someone else who worried about your safety, too."

Herman stared at me.

"What did Mom say to you each time you got up from the chair or the bed?"

"She said, 'Be careful—take your walker—don't fall.'"

"That's right. All Mom cared about was you."

"What do you think Mom would want me to do now?" Herman asked.

"I think you know, Dad. What would she tell you?"

"She'd say, 'Don't be foolish. Go where you'll have help!'"

I wiped Herman's tears and mine.

A NEW HOME

THE MORNING AFTER HERMAN'S AGREEMENT TO move to a long-term care community, the director of admissions of the Shalom Center knocked on his door. Miraculously a bed had opened up in this remarkable nursing facility just as we needed it. The complex could provide not only excellent medical care, but healing religious and cultural opportunities as well.

"Hello, Mr. Liss, I'm Diane Burns from the Shalom Center. May I come in?"

"Please," he said.

"Mr. Liss," said Diane, extending her hand, "I had the pleasure of meeting you two years ago. You and your daughter toured the Shalom Center with me when your wife was ill and in the hospital. I'm sorry to learn about her passing."

"Thank you. May she rest in peace," answered my father. " My wife died a month ago."

I could tell that he had no recollection of meeting Diane or seeing the Shalom Center.

"Mr. Liss, I know this is a difficult time for you, and I promise that at the Shalom Center we will do all we can to help."

"The doctors don't think I should return home. I thought that was what my wife wanted, but maybe it's not," Dad said haltingly.

"Above all, Mom wanted Dad to be safe," I explained, hoping to boost my father's resolve.

"You will be safe, Mr. Liss, and you'll be well cared for. I know that you have always kept kosher and that your faith means so much to you.

The Shalom Center serves kosher food and we hold Sabbath, weekday, and holiday services in our chapel."

"Dad, you'll be able to say *Kaddish* for Mom, and I'll be able to join you."

He shook his head yes.

"The Shalom Center provides support that will be important in your recovery. We have a doctor who will oversee your care, excellent nurses, physical therapists, and aides to assist when you shower and dress. You'll have a safety cord to pull whenever you need help."

"Dad, this sounds wonderful."

He bit his lip.

"Mr. Liss, when you're feeling stronger, the Shalom Center offers outings and entertainment."

Dad looked dazed. I guessed what he was thinking. Plays, music, dining out—that was what he did with Betty. His wife was gone, and so was the joy.

Herman put out his hand to Diane, shook hers, and murmured, "Thank you." He closed his eyes.

Diane understood that Herman was ready for her to leave. As she picked up her bag she said, "Mr. Liss, we're getting a bed set for you for this afternoon. Michele can bring some of your clothes over before you arrive. We invite you to bring pictures and whatever will make you feel at home."

My father rested, and I drove to Revere to gather the items he would need immediately. It had been four weeks since Dad's stroke, and that long since I had been in the home my parents shared. Turning the key to the apartment, seeing my mother's burned-out memorial candle, finding everything just as we had left it, I broke down.

"Mom," I cried out. "How am I going to get through this? Dad's so sick. It happened so fast. What am I going to do? Help me, Mom— please help me."

I sobbed for the first time since my mother's death. The view of the ocean, the smiling pictures, her robe on the sofa evoked memories that broke through the protective barrier of my numbness.

I longed for my mother—just wanted her to hold me. Clutching her robe, I buried my face in its folds. Waves of sorrow rocked me as I lay on the floor in a fetal position and wept.

I GLANCED at the clock. Nearly an hour had passed, and I had to get Dad's clothes and at least a few familiar items for his room. Zombie-like, I gathered pajamas, underwear, shirts, pants and socks. I'd be back for more. Soon, I knew, I'd have to clean out the apartment, make it available for someone else to start a new life in this precious spot.

I drove to the Shalom Center, located just a few miles from my own home. When I arrived the receptionist informed me that my father had come minutes before. She directed me to his room.

"Herman, welcome to the Shalom Center," I heard coming from behind the curtain pulled around Dad's bed. I waited outside the room, scanning it through the open door.

"My name is Carla, and I'm going to be your nurse. I'll be taking care of you during the days. I'm so glad that you're with us, and I think in time you will be, too." Her voice was rich and warm. "May I take your blood pressure, Herman?"

The room was flooded with light. There was a picture window overlooking a grove of trees, just above the second bed on the opposite side of the room. In the middle of the wall, opposite my father, was a blank bulletin board. *That will be perfect for some of Dad's pictures,* I thought. There was a bureau on which to sit a few personal treasures and a narrow, inset closet next to that. Dad's wardrobe would never fit.

When the curtain was pulled back, I saw that the woman was as welcoming as her voice. Her smile, her eyes were kind and reassuring. We shook hands. Carla introduced herself and invited me to spend time with my father and speak with her later that afternoon.

"There'll be others coming to meet you both. If you have any questions, anything you need, please feel free to ask." She went over to my Dad, patted his shoulder and said, "Herman, I'm so happy you've chosen the Shalom Center."

"Thank you," my father said, looking as disoriented as I felt.

"Hi Dad," I said with forced enthusiasm. "I think we made a good decision. It will take time, I know, but people seem very kind. Really, we're so lucky that you were accepted here right from the rehab. I've heard that it can take up to a year to get a bed here. I think Mom's watching out for us."

Herman blinked back tears.

"I brought a few of your things to get you started, and tomorrow I'll go back and get some more."

Dad took my hand and kissed it. "Thank you," he said.

There was a knock on the door. A young woman entered and approached Dad respectfully, gently.

"Hello, Mr. Liss. I'm Lisa Dale, your social worker at the Shalom Center." Dad extended his hand, which Lisa took in both of hers. "We're going to work together as a team with you and your daughter to make the Shalom Center a good home for you."

As Lisa spoke, something about her seemed so familiar. I knew her, but from where?

When she gave me her card, I remembered. Nine months earlier, as a student social worker, Lisa had come to the Satter House with her mentor to do a home care study for Betty and Herman. This young woman had impressed me even then.

"Lisa, we met in Revere, in my parents' apartment.

"Yes," she replied. "I met both your Mom and Dad. I'm so sorry to hear about Mrs. Liss."

"My wife, may she rest in peace. I'm glad that you met her."

"I remember her well. That was a very special visit for me. You see, it was my first home care needs study, and I was so nervous. You both welcomed me so warmly and made me laugh. By the time I left, *I* was feeling much better!"

There was another knock on the door. My father's new aide came to meet him and to explain the safety-call system. Lisa and I spoke privately.

"Lisa, how long have you worked here?"

"Actually, I've just recently joined the staff. Can you believe that your father is my first admission?"

I got the chills. Maybe Mom really was orchestrating this move.

"Lisa, Herman misses my mother terribly. He's in agony."

"We'll get him the support he needs. I promise you."

As we stood on either side of the doorway and spoke, an elderly gentleman, grumbling to himself, pushed his walker between us.

Lisa said, "Hi, Mr. Sacks. This is Michele, your new roommate's daughter. Your roommate's name is Herman."

Mr. Sacks rushed past us with a "Got to go, damn it!" and raced into the bathroom.

"I'll leave you now so you can help your father get settled," Lisa said. "I'll check on Herman later and bring him to the dining room. If there is anything, anything at all that you need, please just find me. My office is right down the hall."

The bathroom door opened and Mr. Sacks shuffled into the room, leaning hard on the walker. He sat on the high-backed chair diagonally across from Herman's bed.

"Mr. Sacks, I'd like you to meet my father, Herman Liss. Dad, this is Mr. Sacks, your roommate."

"Attorney Sacks," I was corrected. "Professor of law."

"How do you do," Herman said.

"What happened to you?" responded Attorney Sacks.

My father looked at me.

"Herman had a stroke about a month ago."

"So, are you here for good, or are you going home?"

Again my father looked at me.

"This is my father's new home," I answered, wondering how this could possibly work.

"Too bad. My kids dumped me here, too. You won't like it. The food's lousy, and no one comes when you call."

My blood pressure was rising. "We've already met some wonderful people. They were very kind," I asserted, as much for myself as my Dad.

"Yeah, just wait. You'll see! What kind of work do you do?" he asked me.

"I was a special educator. I'm taking a break for a while."

"My son is a successful business man, an executive, a big shot."

"Oh, you must be very proud of him," I said, relieved not to hear the complaints.

"I sent him to the best schools!"

"Does he live near here?"

"Nah, he's down south."

"Does he get to visit often?"

"Visit. What's that? He's very busy!"

"Do you have other children?"

"I have a daughter."

"Does she live closer?"

"Yeah, but I don't see her much either."

My father's eyes were closed.

"What did he do?" Attorney Sacks asked, pointing his chin at my father.

"Herman was a regional manager for a food distributor."

The professor sniffed in response. His eyes closed, too.

I put my father's clothes away, kissed him, and wished him a good night.

"I'll see you tomorrow," I whispered as I rubbed the top of his head. "I love you."

"I love you, too," Dad answered. "Thank you."

THE NEXT MORNING I arrived with more clothes and some pictures for the walls and bureaus. Herman was sitting up in bed.

"Good morning, Dad. How did you sleep?"

"OK."

"Did you enjoy your breakfast?"

"It was good."

"Dad, I brought some decorations from home to make your room more comfortable."

"Can I talk to you?" he replied, looking distressed.

Oh, my God, I wondered. *Is he going to tell me he wants to go back to the Satter House?* We were alone in the room, and I sat on his bed and held his hand.

"I think I made a terrible mistake."

My heart sank.

"I'm very worried," he began. "I can't stop thinking about it."

"What's wrong, Dad?"

"You know Mom is buried here—in Massachusetts."

"Yes, that's right."

"I'm going to be buried in Connecticut."

"Yes, I know."

"I can't get it out of my mind. I should have agreed to be buried here, too," he stammered.

Dad continued, "Whenever we talked about the cemetery, Mom would get very upset. She didn't want to be buried in New Haven in my family plot. After my first wife died, I bought a plot for Eva and one for me, right next to where my parents were buried. I didn't think that I'd ever marry again."

"Over the years I told Mom that I wanted to buy a plot for her there, too, but she'd get very upset. She wanted us to be buried together somewhere else. I should have understood, but I thought that I had an obligation to my first wife, too. After a while we stopped talking about it rather than argue. We just couldn't agree.

"I was wrong. Mom wanted to be with me, not with me and another wife. Now Mom is alone in a women's cemetery, and we won't be together, ever again."

"Dad," I said, kissing his forehead, "one day you and Mom will be together again. It doesn't matter where you are buried. It's only the bodies that go into the ground. Your souls will be reunited."

"Nobody knows," he wept.

DARK NIGHT

THE FOLLOWING MORNING AS I APPROACHED MY father's room, I heard banging.

"Herman, hurry up. Get out of there! I got to go!"

"I'm sorry," replied my father. "You'll have to wait or use the bathroom in the hall."

"I can't wait," bellowed Attorney Sacks. "This damn medication makes me go." He nearly rammed me with his walker as I turned into the room.

In a moment the water ran in the sink, and my father opened the door.

"Dad, you shouldn't have gotten up from the toilet without help. It's hard for you to get your balance. Please, from now on pull the safety cord and the aide will come to help you. Do you remember that yesterday she showed you how to call for help?"

"I don't want to bother anyone."

"Well, you're here so you can get the help you need. Promise me that you'll pull the cord from now on."

"Thank you—I will."

When I helped Dad back into bed he said, "While I was in the bathroom my roommate wanted me to come out. I couldn't. He was very angry. You know, he seems upset with everyone. The nurses come to help him, and he yells at them that they didn't come fast enough. I feel bad for them."

"Dad, maybe living with you Attorney Sacks will learn to be more considerate."

"It's important," Herman said, "to treat everyone the way you want to be treated. We all deserve respect."

HERMAN DIDN'T just talk about respect—he lived it. He knew how to listen. He looked into your eyes and into your heart. "Thank you" was readily on his lips. Just being with Herman, people felt appreciated, special, seen. "He's such a gentleman," everyone always said.

Nurses and aides, custodians and administrators, therapists and dining room attendants and other residents stopped me in the hall those first few weeks just to share a Herman story. With genuine amazement and a grateful smile they'd say, "Your father asks me questions about myself and my family," or "Herman wants to know what it's like for me living in America, so far away from home," or "I feel like I've known Herman forever."

The staff was truly multinational. They came from Colombia, Vietnam, India, the Philippines, Africa, Puerto Rico, the Caribbean, Mexico, Russia, and the U.S. Descriptions of Herman tumbled in an array of accents: intelligentgentlebigheartedwarmkindsensitivesweet-thoughtfulhandsomestrongdignifiedfunny.

Herman, living with pain, with grief, with loss, was still Herman.

Dad's mornings were filled with religious services, an array of therapies, a shower, and a rest before lunch. We spent the afternoons together—talking, sharing, and reminiscing. I read the papers and news magazines to him, as since his stroke the letters slid across the page. World and local events had always fascinated Herman, and he delighted in analyzing motives, making predictions, and reflecting on history to illuminate the present. Although my father's speech had slowed, his reasoning and reflections remained rich.

Invariably Herman's thoughts turned to Betty. "Each time I close my eyes I see her breathing hard, her mouth twisted. What if she's still like that?"

My reassurances did little to soothe him.

Again and again Herman lamented about his choice of burial site. "It's too late now," he'd say. "Mom is in a women's cemetery, alone."

Thinking that I could break through the grief-laden images, I brought in pictures of my mother when she was joyful and healthy— pictures of the two of them on boats, on camels, dancing in the moonlight. They only made him miss her more.

Three months after Herman's arrival at the Shalom Center, my phone rang late at night. "Michele, this is Mary, your father's nurse. It's not an emergency, but your father fell getting out of bed. He didn't call for help. He begged me not to tell you, didn't want you to worry, but we have to report falls to family."

"Is he hurt?"

"He fell on his shoulder and his knee, but he says he's all right."

Just as Herman never wanted to disturb anyone, so too, did he not want to cause worry. Even if he were hurt, he wouldn't complain.

The following morning I brought a bold sign that said "PULL CORD FOR SAFETY!" As I hung it on his bulletin board I pleaded with him to call for help whenever he got up. "Promise me, Dad, please."

"Thank you, I will," he said.

"How is your shoulder?"

"It's OK," he replied.

I touched it and he winced. It was obvious that the pain in his arthritic knee was even worse. We walked down the long hall to the dining room for dinner, Herman stopping every few feet to rest. He was breathing hard.

After I helped him get seated, I spoke to the physician's assistant. "I'm concerned about my father," I said. "He's in a lot of pain from his fall, and I know he's not telling you."

"We'll have an X-ray taken of his shoulder and knee, and I'll ask the doctor to prescribe a mild painkiller. He shouldn't have to be uncomfortable."

That evening the medication was begun. Within two days there were dramatic changes. Herman was hallucinating. He reported visits from friends he hadn't seen in decades. Herman was creating sales strategies for the cookie business. My father had forgotten that all of his sisters had died. He slept most of the day and lost his appetite.

"The pain medication must be the cause," I suggested to his nurse.

"It's such a low dose, that's not likely, but we can try something else."

"Oh, please," I said, eager to have my father back.

Although rare, the new medication merely worsened the symptoms.

A few days later I met with my father's team. It was decided to take him off of the pain pills and put him in a room across from the nurses' station and near the dining room. The need to walk and, hopefully, the resulting pain would be reduced. We agreed that I'd be the one to discuss this with him.

"Dad, would it be OK with you if you were to be moved closer to the nurses' station? Help can come even sooner, and you won't have to walk as far to eat."

"Will Carla still be my nurse?"

"No, she's the nurse on this side of the hall. You'll have a new nurse."

"Carla is so good to me, I hate to leave her. And what about my roommate? I don't want him to think I'm leaving because of him."

"You'll still be on this floor, and Carla plans to see you every day. We can explain the situation to Attorney Sacks. I know you've become friends, but you'll be together in the dining room, and you can visit in your room or in the coffee shop. He'll understand."

"What do you think? Do you think I should do this?"

"Yes, it's important."

"OK, I'll move. But you spent so much time decorating this room. It's going to be a lot of work for you."

"Dad, don't worry. I'll be glad to do it again. The other room faces the front, and you'll have an even better view. Lisa says that your new roommate is a great guy. You'll enjoy each other's company."

"Thank you," Dad replied.

THE FOLLOWING MORNING Herman's room was changed, and he was taken off the pain medication. Within days Herman was sitting by the window and reading the newspaper.

"My double vision is gone. The letters aren't jumping off the page. I can read again!" Dad exclaimed.

In the new room I hung the pictures of the dancing rabbis, the scene of the binding of Isaac embroidered by Herman's mother, Moses receiving the Ten Commandments, and his parents' portraits. We decorated the bureaus with family pictures and mementos from Herman and Betty's trips.

Each morning I went to Revere to pack, and in the afternoon I'd bring a different small treasure to add to Dad's collection. It was mid-

January and the Satter House apartment had to be empty by the end of the month.

"Before you close the apartment I want to go back, one last time," Dad implored.

Each bureau and cabinet and closet that I emptied deepened my sadness, and I wanted to spare Herman that pain. "Dad, I've brought everything that's important to you. You just have to tell me if there's anything I missed. I'll find it and bring that, too."

"I really have to see what's left of my clothes, and there may be some important papers still there. I might want something I can't remember," Herman pleaded.

"I'm concerned that making the trip will be exhausting for you."

"I'll be all right. I need to go back. Please!"

My throat closed. "OK, Dad. I'll ask David to help us. We'll go the day after tomorrow. We'll borrow a wheelchair so you won't have to walk into the building or down the hall."

"No," he insisted. "I can do it. I can walk."

THE DAY OF OUR TRIP Herman was weak, shaky, and subdued. He sat in the front seat next to David, and I sat in the back with my hands on his shoulders.

When we arrived, David took the walker from the trunk while I lowered Dad's feet onto the ground. We supported my father's six-foot frame as he maneuvered out of his seat and found his balance against the walker. I held the back of his belt to bolster him, and David placed his hands on the walker to help push it. The three of us walked in tandem. Dad's breath was labored, and the pain in his knees flashed across his face.

When I opened the apartment door, there was silence. It was the first time Herman had been back since Betty's passing and his stroke three months earlier.

A few steps in, Dad gazed at the hall closet, his voice quivering. "I'd like to look at my clothes first."

David placed a chair in front of the closet and said, "I have to go back to work for a bit. Will two hours be enough time for you to finish?"

Herman nodded his head. "Thank you," he whispered.

While my father sat, I pulled out each remaining shirt, jacket, and tie for him to hold. He caressed every one.

"Mom bought this tie," Dad said. "Whenever we shopped Betty would always find something for me. She'd tell me, 'This color is good for you. You'll wear it when we go out.' I really didn't need anything more, but it made her happy." Dad cradled each item as it told its story. He found his favorite tie, a navy one with delicate, leaping orange carp. "Mom loved this one," he recalled. She always said that fish are lucky."

After selecting a few more shirts and ties and two more jackets, Dad asked to lie down. "I need to rest for a while. Do you mind?"

Herman and I pushed the walker into the bedroom and over to the lonely twin bed against the wall. He sat and I lifted his legs up onto the mattress.

"Thank you," Dad said as he laid back. "I just need to close my eyes for a while."

"Rest, Dad," I replied, kissing his cheek and smoothing his hair.

As Herman slept, I sorted his remaining clothes and heard Mom's voice in the distance. "Sweetheart, wear this shirt with these pants. They go so well together. You'll look so handsome."

"Michele," Dad called after a while. "Can you please come here?"

I sat on his bed and held his hand.

"Michele, I have something to ask you." His speech was steady, calm, resolved. "Can you help me, please? Is there anything you can give me so I can join Mom? I shouldn't be here without her. It's not right. I was ten years older. I should have gone first. Please, help me."

Oh, no! Did I understand? *What do I do? What do I say?* Groping for time, for words, I asked, "Tell me, Dad, what are you thinking?"

"Maybe there's a pill you can give me. I've lived my life. There's no more for me to do. There is no reason for me to be here. I just want to be with my sweetheart—now."

"Dad," I began, my heart pounding in my ears, "I understand how you feel. I know you miss Mom. I miss her, too, and it hurts. But it's not up to us to make this decision."

Desperate, I went on. "I believe that Mom is with us, watching over us, and when the time is right, you will be together again. This is just not the time. There must be a very important reason that you are here. It may not feel that way to you now. But there is."

I excused myself, went into the bathroom, and opened the medicine cabinet. I removed a full month's supply of OxyContin, hiding it in my jacket.

When I returned I moved silently next to Herman, watching his tears trail a path toward his ears. On the bureau was a photo of Mom and Dad beaming, dancing joyously at their grandson's wedding. Frozen, I stood sentinel holding Herman's hand until David arrived with a wheelchair. This time Herman didn't refuse.

Lisa was at the nurses' station when we arrived at the Shalom Center. "Herman, you must be tired. Would you like to have dinner in your room tonight?"

"No, thank you. I'm not hungry. I just need to lie down."

After we settled Dad in his room, I walked to the desk. "Lisa, I need to talk to you."

"It must have been a very difficult visit," she offered.

"It was. Herman misses my Mom desperately and sees no reason to live. He just asked me to help him die. I'm the only one he shares these feelings with. He needs to be able to talk to someone—someone with experience who can listen and help him cope."

"Yes, you're right. Herman's been seeing our psychologist, but he hasn't opened up. We have a psychiatrist who can evaluate him. I'll call him tomorrow."

"Please, Lisa—I'm very worried."

"We'll get him the right help. I promise."

LATE THE FOLLOWING MORNING I received a call from Lisa. She sounded nervous. "The psychiatrist saw Herman and is having him admitted to the local hospital's geriatric psychiatry unit. We feel that he needs to be on a twenty-four hour watch for a while. He told the psychiatrist the same thing he told you. Herman asked for help in dying."

"Lisa, I don't think he'd hurt himself. He's grieving. Can't he receive psychiatric help at the Shalom Center?"

"We need to know he's safe and that he's of no risk to himself. The hospital will be able to evaluate him for medication and recommend therapy. He shouldn't be hospitalized for long. I'm sorry, Michele."

"I'll be right there. I want to be the one to tell him."

"Please hurry, because the ambulance will be here by noon."

I entered Dad's room to find him sitting, staring out the window. "Dad, you're going to be going to the hospital for a few days, just to be checked out."

"What do you mean? I'm not sick. I don't need to be in a hospital."

I was at a loss. I couldn't say, "Dad, they're sending you because they're afraid you might take your life!"

So instead I bluffed. "You've fallen a few times recently, and your shoulder still hurts. They just want to check you out to make sure you're OK. The doctors want to know if you need any more treatment."

My father's new nurse, Lori, came in and hugged him. "Herman, I've only known you a few days, but I'm really going to miss you." She kissed his cheek. "You'll be back soon."

Herman looked at her forlornly. "I've never been evicted before."

The ambulance attendants arrived and strapped Herman to a stretcher, covering him with the too familiar white hospital blanket. *Not again,* I thought. "I'll meet you at the hospital, Dad. I love you."

I gathered some clothes and a few personal items to bring with me. When I arrived at the hospital and gave my father's name, the volunteer whispered, "There's only one elevator that goes to that floor. For security reasons you have to call on the phone outside of the elevator and tell them the name of the patient and your relationship. The nurse will then punch in a special code that allows the elevator to stop there. When you exit the elevator you must call on the phone outside of the locked unit and request that they buzz you in."

My heart sank. How could this be? My sweet, gentle father was in a locked ward!

I followed directions and called on the phone outside of the unit to request entrance. I waited as the nurse checked my authority to visit. The buzzer sounded and I pushed open a heavy metal door.

The nurse stood and held out her hand. "I'll have to take that bag from you. I need to check it before you can take it to the patient."

I handed her the plastic bag. She dumped it out and saw the clothing and shaving kit. "I'll have to keep the razor and the belt," she said. "When he's discharged you can have them back."

Did she think my ninety-three-year-old father who couldn't balance was going to hang himself with his belt? "Your father is in Room 10, straight ahead and to the right."

It was the longest walk of my life.

For a full week Herman attended group and individual psycho-therapy sessions, art therapy, music therapy, and cinema therapy. He had brain scans and blood tests. A psychiatrist, psychologist, and psychiatric social worker evaluated him.

"Why am I here?" he kept asking me. "Are they going to let me go back to the Shalom Center? Will I have my same room? How long do I have to stay?"

"Yes, Dad, you'll be going back to your own room at the Shalom Center, and it should be soon. The doctors here will be able to tell your own doctors what you need to get well. You've been through so much with Mom's passing and then your stroke. The Shalom Center wants to know that they are providing you with the best care."

"I just want to go back."

A week after Dad was admitted, the chief psychiatrist met with me to review the findings.

"Your father is an exceptional gentleman, intelligent and insightful. Herman is exhibiting an understandable deep grief reaction to his wife's passing. He is of absolutely no danger to himself. In fact, he told each of us that he knows that life is a gift and that the time of our passing is up to God.

"The stroke has slowed blood flow to the brain so speech and memory are affected, but that hasn't impacted his ability to think. I'm prescribing a new medication to slow memory loss, along with an antidepressant that is especially effective in the elderly."

The doctor continued, "Herman has two primary problems. He is in profound despair over losing your mother, and he feels that his life has no purpose."

I was certain the answers to these problems weren't going to be found in just those two little pills. Yes, they might brighten his mood and help him remember names, but that wasn't enough. "Thank you, doctor. I appreciate your help. May I take him home today?"

"Yes, Herman is officially discharged."

"Can we leave now?" Dad asked eagerly when I got to his room.

"Right now, Dad. Right now!"

"Please," he said, "don't ever let me come back here!"

"I promise, Dad. It will never happen."

I made another promise, this one to myself. Somehow Herman would discover meaning and purpose in his new life, and find the hope that one day he and his sweetheart might dance together again.

WELCOME HOME

"WELCOME BACK, HERMAN!" SHOUTED LORI, his young nurse, as she ran down the hall and threw her arms around his neck. "I missed you so much!"

"Oh, I missed you, too! It's so good to be back!"

"You're home now, Herman," Lori said as she kissed him.

"Yes," he grinned. "Home."

"You've been out in the cold. How would you like some hot packs for your knees? I'll bring them to your room, and we can talk before you go to lunch."

"I'd like that very much. Thank you."

Herman sighed as he settled onto his bed, and Lori wrapped the warm packs around his achy joints. "You know, Herman, if there's anything you need, please call me. Pull the cord. I'll come running."

"Thank you," Herman said. "And if I can help you in any way, I want you to tell me."

"I promise, Herman, I will."

In the short time we had before lunch, I unpacked Dad's clothes and told him there would be a surprise when he came back from the dining room.

While Herman was in the hospital I began to wonder—must life remain dark and meaningless after loss, even near the end of life? Is it possible for there to be joy, laughter, and hope? And what about growth and learning? *Why not?* I asked myself.

Soon Herman wheeled his walker down the hall to the dining room, and nurses, aides, and residents shook his hand, hugged him, and welcomed him home. As Dad had his lunch, I went to work.

Out of my backpack I pulled a collection of Halloween pictures taken at the Satter House—photos of Herman in his prize-winning costumes. Up on the bulletin board went the flaxen beauty in Betty's hot pink swimsuit with matching knee braces, looking voluptuous with the aid of gym socks and artfully applied makeup. Herman smiled and waved from every picture. Around these photos I posted Herman as a raven-haired hula dancer in a green grass skirt and Mom's silk turquoise bra. The multi-colored Hawaiian lei coordinated with the flowered covered walker. Pictures of both of my parents framed the bathing beauty and sultry dancer. Herman was dressed as an angel, in a long white gown fringed with white ostrich feathers. A silver halo topped his wavy blond hair. On his walker basket Dad placed a stuffed bear with gossamer wings that matched his own. Betty, dressed as a devil, smiled beside him. It was their last Halloween together.

Dad returned from lunch and saw me putting up the final pictures. The two of us laughed with complete abandon, the way we did when Mom was well. We still knew how!

"What's so funny?" asked Lori as she popped into the room. "I heard you from two doors down."

Herman showed her his "coming out" pictures, and Lori shot back, "Herman, we have a costume party every Halloween here at the Shalom Center. It's always been the staff that gets dressed up for the residents, but would you dress up with me?"

Herman's eyes began to dance.

"Since you make such a gorgeous woman, let's do something they'll never forget. What do you say?"

"Yes, let's do it!"

"OK, Herman, how would you like to dress?"

"Michele, remember what Mom said on our last Halloween?"

"Remind me, Dad."

"Well, she said that next time I should go either as Shirley Temple or—"

"Yes, Dad—" I began to chuckle. "Or what?"

"A call girl!"

"Oh yes, I remember! So what do you think?"

Dad blushed and grinned from ear to ear.

Lori jumped in. "Herman, if you want to go as a hooker, I could dress as your pimp. I have a teenage cousin who could loan me his suit, and I have lots of gold chains to make it look authentic."

"Michele," asked Dad. "Do you think you could put together a costume for me?"

"Of course I can!" We were laughing so hard that we closed the door.

"OK," Lori said. "We have eight months to plan this—not a word to anyone!"

The three of us clasped hands and made our pledge. When Lori left, Herman turned to me and asked, "Do you think this would make Mom happy?"

"Dad, she'll be there cheering for you. She'll love it!"

I was encouraged. We had something joyful to look forward to. *We need more and more of this,* I thought.

That evening I began to imagine activities that could help to bring life back into Dad's world. What might ignite Herman's will to live? What could make him want to get up in the morning, every morning? What would spark his heart and mind and soul?

A thought of my father at prayer emerged. Morning and evening he used to sit with his prayer book intoning the ancient verses. The image was peaceful, purposeful.

Yes, this was the key to reconnect Dad to life. His faith was always the cornerstone of his being—here was meaning for Herman. All right, my father could teach me about our faith. We could learn and grow together.

THE NEXT AFTERNOON I invited Herman to come with me to the Shalom Center coffee shop. "There's something important I'd like to ask you, Dad." I paused. "I've always wanted to learn to read Hebrew, but the religious school I attended as a child didn't do a good job of teaching Hebrew to the girls. The boys had Hebrew tutors before their bar mitzvahs, but the girls' education didn't seem important. Would you teach me, Dad, please?"

My father took my hands and kissed them. "Nothing would make me happier. Yes, I'll teach you. When would you like to start?" His eyes were gleaming.

"Right now, if that's OK. I have a Hebrew primer with me, and I need to start with a review of the letters, if that's all right with you."

"That's wonderful," Dad said. "After you learn the letters and their sounds, we can read together from my prayer book. Would you please go to my room and get my glasses and my yarmulke?"

"I'll be right back!"

EACH AFTERNOON Dad and I studied together. He listened as I struggled to memorize the unfamiliar letters and blend them into words. Patiently he corrected me as I confused those that looked similar. Again and again I'd ask, "How does this one sound?" Regardless of the number of times he had to correct me, he was as gentle and encouraging as if it were the first.

I began attending Friday evening services with my father in the Shalom Center chapel. Dad would keep place on the line so I wouldn't get lost. Soon the baffling characters became my friends. I was able to follow the prayers and songs that in the past I knew only from memory. Now I could read them.

"Mom would be so proud of you," Dad beamed as he squeezed my hand.

He had no idea how proud I was of him.

PART III

MEETING MICHAEL

IN MID-MARCH, A FEW WEEKS AFTER WE BEGAN OUR studies, I arrived for my lesson and found Herman sitting, staring out of the window, his forehead furrowed.

"Hi, Dad. How are you? You look deep in thought. Is everything OK?"

"A boy came to visit me this afternoon. He said he's coming back next week, but I don't know why."

"Who is he, Dad?"

"I don't know who he is. His name is Michael, and he looks to be about twelve or thirteen. But I don't know why he was here or if he's really coming back. He's only a boy. What am I going to do with him?"

"Dad, I'll ask Rebecca about Michael. She must know."

Rebecca, the activity director, explained that Michael was a seventh-grade student at the Marblehead Community Charter Public School. He had a service learning assignment and chose to make a few visits to the Shalom Center to receive his credit.

I returned to Herman and explained that Michael was visiting as part of his course work.

"He seems to be a nice boy, rather shy, didn't say much. I really don't know what I can do for him."

"Just be yourself, Dad. That's all you have to do. That's enough."

MEETING HERMAN
MICHAEL

I FIRST MET HERMAN LISS ON THE 15TH OF MARCH 2003. School had brought me there—it was a community service assignment. That assignment was only supposed to last until the end of the term, and because I had started late, I only had to visit Herman once to fulfill my requirement.

I had tried unsuccessfully many times to find a place to volunteer. Again and again I called a woman who was the head of an elderly housing development that was, incidentally, across the street from my school. I could never get a hold of her. The receptionist and I were soon on a first name basis, and I knew the number by heart. Once I finally spoke with her I learned that she was the wrong person to call. Finally, over February vacation, my mother made the phone call herself and found me a volunteer position at the Shalom Center.

I knew that what I most wanted to do at the Shalom Center was to talk with one of the residents. This was very familiar, as I had already chatted with the elderly at "intergenerational events" at my school. These had only gone on for an hour or so, but the little bits that I had experienced had turned out to be informative, enjoyable, and most of all, powerful. I didn't know what I was going to do, or what I was going to say, but I felt as though I knew enough to improvise. Just talking with someone seemed rather easy, but in practice it can be quite challenging.

I brought up my goals on my first day at the Shalom Center. It's hard for me to remember what volunteering was like before meeting Herman, because I immediately associate everything about the Shalom

Center with him. I remember having to attend an orientation and doing a little bit of administrative work. I stapled papers together and stacked chairs and filled out some forms. All through this I was wondering whether or not they would direct me to one of the residents.

There is one specific pre-Herman incident that I remember. On my first day I sat in the coffee room playing cards with a resident named Ruth. Over in the corner there was an elderly man in a wheelchair with a younger woman. She was reading what looked like a biblical picture storybook. He looked interested, but he seemed distant and distracted—sad, almost. I needed to get back to my card game, though, so I paid him no mind for the rest of the afternoon.

On my fourth Thursday, I was debating whether or not to go to the nursing home. I was scheduled to go for a visit, but I had just finished an exhausting day at school that had been bad in many ways. I called my mom at work, and as I paced through the living room I complained to her that I had no time to volunteer because of a big event coming up at school. She suggested that I go just for the heck of it. "It isn't a big deal, Mike," she said. "You'll just go quickly and ask if they need any help. You'll still have time to do what you need. You'll get to clean up a little after. It'll be fine."

I arrived at the Shalom Center in a bit of a belligerent mood. I couldn't find any of the administrators who were usually there. I walked around confused for some time. I didn't have any idea why I was there or what to do. It was as though someone had put me, at twelve years old, in an airport in Houston and said, "Okay, I'll meet you in Caracas at noon," and then drove away.

The nursing home wasn't quite sure what do with me either. When I finally ran into an administrator, it was pure luck. I asked her what I could do. She thought a while. "Well, I can't think of anything for you to do. No, I think we're all set."

Maybe I could go home now. I was both relieved and frustrated. She paused then, contemplating. "You said you wanted to visit a resident? There's a man here named Herman Liss. He's very sharp and easy to talk to and devout. Do you want to go see him?"

Well, I had managed to buy the tickets for the Houston-Caracas flight, and there had been an announcement that I was boarding. Some progress. What next? And what does "sharp" mean in nursing home terms? Why should I want to speak to someone "devout?" When I pictured the word devout, an old, ragged imam on pilgrimage to Mecca, hands cupped toward the sky, came to mind. It was worth a try, though.

I walked into a dimly lit room. I thought I recognized the man lying down in the bed, but I couldn't remember from where.

"This is Mr. Liss," she said, directing her attention to Herman. "Herman's a very devout man. Right?" Again the pilgrim sprang to mind.

Then I recognized Herman. He was the one who was being read to in the coffee shop a few weeks earlier. Herman had what looked like a very big scab on the right side of his nose. I had noticed it when I first saw him in the coffee shop. I later learned it was a cancerous growth. *Oh, no,* I thought. *How can I look at that every week?* This was the first thought that I had about Herman Liss.

He nodded, agreeing that he was devout. I was uncomfortable, both physically and mentally. I didn't know if sitting on his bed would be impolite, but I really needed to sit down, and I couldn't see any chairs.

"Feel free to sit down on my bed," Herman offered.

Even sitting down there I was uncomfortable, but I didn't feel as though I was in any position to make him move.

He began by telling me that he had had a stroke, and apologized if I wasn't able to hear or understand him. I thought his apology was out of place, as though I would be offended by his voice. His speech sounded fine to me. It was one of the first topics we covered, as if he wanted to get through that quickly to ease his self-consciousness and mine.

Herman began to speak about the Purim festival that was coming up. On Purim, children and adults alike dress up and eat candy and fruit to celebrate the holiday. He was obviously excited about the Shalom Center's upcoming party. To make conversation I told him that for the first time in my memory, this year St. Patrick's Day and Purim would be on the same day.

"The Irishmen and the Jews in this facility are trying to coordinate one big holiday. The Irish are putting up green everywhere, and the Jews are putting up blue. It's sort of a battle of the holidays," he said, laughing.

Pleased that the conversation was going somewhere, I made a joke. "Imagine how many people will be drunk that day!" It had just occurred to me that there is a Jewish law about Purim, saying that you are supposed to get so drunk that you shouldn't be able to tell the difference between the wicked and the wise. And I live in Boston. St. Patrick's Day is big. Many people go into the bars and drink themselves into a stupor.

Herman laughed. "It doesn't matter, though," he said. "There's only one God." He suddenly became very earnest. He looked me straight in the eye.

I had just met Herman Liss and landed at the Simon Bolivar Airport in Caracas.

THE REIGN

WE HAD BEGUN OUR STUDY OF HEBREW IN FEB-ruary, a few weeks before the festival of Purim, a joyful holiday celebrating the victory of good over evil. There are Purim plays, children and adults attend services dressed in costume, and home-baked treats and candies are shared with friends and neighbors. Herman reminisced about the celebrations of his youth, and he eagerly anticipated the festivities at the Shalom Center. Truthfully, I knew little about the history or significance of the holiday, and felt that this would be a perfect opportunity for Herman to teach and for me to learn. I bought an artfully designed book on Jewish history and holidays that stirred my father's rich memories. The staff began to ask Herman to share his stories, and they, too, learned about the customs of so many of their residents.

The week before Purim, the activity director took me aside. "Michele, each Purim we have a holiday celebration during which a King and Queen are selected. Your father has been nominated to be a contestant. Do you think he would agree to be our king?"

"This sounds like fun. Please tell me more!"

"The contestants are asked questions about what the holiday means to them and how they would reign should they be selected as King or Queen for the year. The winners are chosen by applause from the audience and retain the crown until the following year. The party and competition are full of fun, and the royal couple has their picture posted in our display case and published in our newsletter. It's really an honor."

"I think Herman would love it, and I'd like you to be the one to ask him," I said.

"I'll go speak with him right now," Rebecca replied.

On the day of the party over one hundred residents and the entire staff gathered in the downstairs lobby. The staff, dressed as the characters in the Purim story, performed a Purim play, and then the nominees for King and Queen were brought to the front of the room. Each was asked questions about the meaning of the holiday and how they would treat their "subjects" should they be selected.

When it was Herman's turn he said that if chosen, "respect" would be the watchword of his reign. "We need to treat each other just as we want to be treated."

"And," asked Rebecca, "Herman, how can we make the Shalom Center an even happier place?"

Herman's smile was warm and broad. He answered, "To me, happiness means appreciating all of the good in your own life—and helping to make life good for others."

The cheers for him were heartfelt.

Herman's Queen, Rachel, was as beautiful as he was handsome. In her late eighties, Rachel was straight, tall, and fashionable. She had been a beauty queen in her younger years. Dressed in a bright purple suit with coordinating brooch and antique earrings, she exuded poise and charm.

What a regal pair! The coronation portrait with King and Queen draped in red velvet robes and wearing gold colored crowns hung in the lobby for the year. The King kissed the Queen's hand. Respect reigned.

Our Second Visit

Michael

THERE. **I** HAD FULFILLED MY COMMUNITY SERVICE requirement. I know that sounds like I just came out of jail, but really, it was just a term thing for school. I didn't have to worry about it anymore. Next trimester we'd be picking vegetables out of the garden and giving them to charity. That sounded easy enough.

Which is why it may seem odd that I went back to visit Herman for a second time. Later on people would ask why I came back. To this day I don't have a definite answer. It just seemed like the right thing to do.

I walked into the Shalom Center and tried to remember Herman's room number. Should I go back and visit, or should I report to Rebecca and help her in the office? *"But it doesn't matter, there's only one God—"* I heard in my head.

I began to walk down the hall to Herman.

After a few visits I learned I could find Herman reading in one of three places—in his room facing the window, in the coffee shop, or in the community room. I checked the coffee shop and there he was, with the woman who had been reading to him before.

"Herman," I said, not wanting to startle him.

Herman barely knew me, but his face lit up and he greeted me as if I had known him for years. "This is my daughter, Michele. She's a real doll. Michele, this is the volunteer I was telling you about. Please sit down—take a chair."

I was excited that day because later on I would be missing school to fly to Disney World for my sister's dance performance. Eagerly I explained what was going on to Michele and Herman.

I noticed that I felt more relaxed in that atmosphere with Herman than in most other places. Here I could talk about anything without fearing ridicule. Had I gone on like this about my Disney World vacation, sounding like an excited four-year-old, to someone my age, I would hear from them "Alert the media!" "So what?" "No shit, Sherlock!"

How nice to simply be able to talk. This comfort continued until the very last day.

THE INVITATION

MICHAEL'S VISITS DIDN'T STOP AFTER TWO WEEKS, much to our surprise. Herman, with increasing exuberance, described their conversations and activities. "You know, Michael is really coming into his own. He's very intelligent, and talented, too. He's not shy anymore. What a boy! He's wise beyond his years."

Weekly I heard stories about this remarkable child who knew and cared about current events and politics and religion. Most of all, he cared about his friend. After each visit my father would exclaim, "Today Michael played the piano for me," or "This afternoon Michael shared his cartooning," or "Michael took me for a walk in the garden."

The eighty-year age difference didn't seem to matter. A twelve-year-old was bringing Herman back to life.

In early May, just a few weeks after they met, my father handed me a heavy, cream-colored envelope. It was addressed to Herman.

"Dad, what's this?"

"Open it," he beamed.

"Wow, an invitation to Michael's bar mitzvah!"

"Yes, he wants us to come, both of us! Do you think we can?"

"Of course we'll go, Dad. What an honor! Michael must adore you!"

"He's fond of you, too," Dad replied. "I look forward to meeting Michael's parents. They must be wonderful people. Look how they're raising him!"

For the next six weeks Herman's excitement built. Exercise classes and physical therapy sessions now had a purpose. He was getting

AN END OF LIFE STORY WITHOUT END

stronger, becoming fit for Michael's bar mitzvah. Herman's anticipation evoked memories of the first time he was called to the Torah. He mused about the preparation, his family's joy, and the meaning of his own coming of age passage eight decades earlier.

Days before Michael's bar mitzvah, Herman chose the suit and tie he planned to wear. He meticulously brushed his pinstripe suit and hung his leaping fish tie beside it. Next he polished his gleaming black leather shoes. Finally he caressed the blue velvet bag that held his prayer shawl. Lovingly he placed it on the top of his bureau. He was ready!

On Saturday morning I arrived early to help my father finish dressing. How handsome he was! I watched as he checked his breast-pocket handkerchief in the mirror, certain that I glimpsed Herman's reflection on his own bar mitzvah day.

MICHAEL LED THE SERVICE with poise and skill. Herman mouthed every prayer along with him, smiling and nodding as Michael completed each passage. He sat transfixed during Michael's speech that expanded on the meaning of the Torah portion he read in Hebrew.

Following the service Herman met Michael's mother and father, sister and grandmother. *"Mazel Tov!* Congratulations! You must be so proud of Michael!"

Herman clearly was.

Our Bar Mitzvah

Michael

AFTER MANY VISITS WITH HERMAN, I BEGAN TO wonder—but was never brave enough to ask—did he ever leave the nursing home? Or did his health not allow that? The thought of Herman being almost trapped, when I knew he used to travel the world, was an awful thought.

Soon Herman had an opportunity to go out, because my bar mitzvah was coming up. The thought of inviting him as a friend excited me. This was the first feeling of genuine pride I had since meeting him, because I knew that the combination of Herman's Judaism and the opportunity to get out would make this the perfect invitation. I decided to hand deliver the invitation to him. I could hardly wait.

When I first asked Herman to attend my bar mitzvah, he wasn't quite sure what I was doing. I came in, very eager to hand him the envelope with the invitation enclosed. I wondered if he would be able to make it. Though even if he couldn't, I felt proud nonetheless.

I gave Herman the envelope addressed especially to him, and he looked curiously at it for a while. "So, we have an RSVP card in here somewhere—" I explained.

Herman finally understood. "You're inviting me?" he said, beaming. A few months ago he wasn't even sure why I was there. Now I was inviting him to my bar mitzvah, and he was beginning to understand—I was there to be his friend. "Thank you, thank you!"

He proudly signed his name on the RSVP card. He said he would attend the service in the synagogue, but not the kid-oriented party at night at the catering hall. This didn't surprise me.

THE MORNING of my bar mitzvah, as I read the Mourner's *Kaddish,* I looked over to Herman in the back row. He was reading along to a sacred prayer that I knew meant so much to him—the prayer in which he honored his wife's memory. It was difficult to stand on the pulpit and pay proper attention to everyone, so I didn't watch Herman as much as I would have liked. I had to concentrate on reading all I had to read, and saying whatever I had to say. I did catch a glimpse of a beaming Herman every now and then, however.

I learned later that my bar mitzvah in June 2003 was the first major outing Herman had had since he entered the Shalom Center in the fall of 2002. I feel that the main reason he looked so happy at my bar mitzvah was because he was watching me in one of the most important events in my life as a Jew. He was watching me become happy. This in turn made him happy.

The bar mitzvah was the first big deal that deepened the relationship between Herman and me. I had sent Herman a postcard from Disney World, but other than that we only talked. After the bar mitzvah Herman felt sorry that he couldn't come to my party, so to make up for it he and Michele invited my parents, my sister, Allie, and me to a picnic in honor of my bar mitzvah. We celebrated in the Shalom Center's community room.

We showed Herman the video of the bar mitzvah party, and he watched with great interest. He had gone to many parties in his day, many of which were at Jewish resorts in the Catskill Mountains.

Over our meal he told me stories about going to boxing matches and submitting 100 words to newspapers for which he wrote, and stories of his business career. It really seemed as though someone else should hear this besides me.

THE SOUL'S JOURNEY

HERMAN'S LIFE WAS GROWING RICHER AS HE ENjoyed frequent visits from our family, my friends, and his young companion, Michael. The staff and other residents treasured him. Learning and sharing enlivened his days, and life, once more, had meaning.

Still, there were flickers of sadness—a far off gaze, a catch in Herman's voice, a longing. Eight months after Betty's death, his choice of burial site continued to haunt him. Above all, Herman yearned to know, was his beloved safe?

On the day Herman was discharged from the psychiatric unit, I made two promises. First was to help him rediscover a reason to live. He did. The second was to help him know peace. This proved to be more challenging.

Although my father was a man of deep faith who lived and practiced the ethics of Judaism, his soul ached. Where was Betty? Was she all right? Might they ever be reunited? Traditional Jewish education and religious experiences rarely explore the soul's journey. Do we simply return to dust or is there more? Is there any reason to hope?

I began a search for a text by a learned rabbi that explored the Jewish concept of soul, and obsessively combed libraries, bookstores, and the Internet. The answer came a few weeks later in the mail. A simple catalogue from a small press, Jewish Lights in Woodstock, Vermont, featured a book entitled *Does the Soul Survive? A Jewish Journey to Belief in Afterlife, Past Lives and Living With Purpose.*

Amazing! This might be the key! The description asked, "Do we have a soul that survives an earthly existence? Near-death experiences? Channeling the dead? Is this sort of thing Jewish?" Best of all, the author, Rabbi Elie Kaplan Spitz, is a scholar who specializes in spirituality and Judaism, a rabbi who is also a lawyer and a teacher of philosophy of Jewish law. What could be better? Rabbi Spitz, a member of the Rabbinical Assembly Committee of Law and Standards, was certainly a learned man.

When I read *Does the Soul Survive?* I was astonished. This one source offered even more than I could have imagined—an integration of biblical text, ancient writings, and an introduction to Jewish mysticism and Kabbalah. It featured research on past life regression and near-death phenomena, and explored Jewish references to mediumship. All of this was interwoven with Rabbi Spitz's personal mystical experiences. Here was hope. Here was the missing piece!

With unrestrained enthusiasm I presented Herman with the book, disclosing its message.

"Thank you," replied my father, his response more subdued than my description.

"Dad, as you read it can we talk about it, maybe chapter by chapter?"

"All right. I'll start it tonight."

The next afternoon I found my father sitting by the window absorbed in his reading. He looked up, removed his glasses, and said, "Rabbi Spitz believes that after someone dies the body goes into the ground with all its infirmities, and the healthy soul unites with God."

"What do you think, Dad?"

"How can we know for sure? No one has come back to report."

"Dad, as you read on, you'll see that many people throughout the world have been rescued from clinical death. Their reports are amazingly similar. They often describe being met by loved ones who had passed on before them. It's common to hear of travel through a long, dark tunnel leading to a brilliant, love-filled light."

"Yes, but how do we know it's real? How do we know they actually saw this?"

"That's a good question, Dad. Now let me ask *you* something."

"All right."

"Has anyone ever come back to report that they've seen God?"

"Not that I know of."

"So, how can we believe?"

Herman pondered, chewed his lip. After a long silence he said, "Faith. Simple faith."

Each afternoon Herman and I sat in the coffee shop overlooking the gardens and debated the possibility of life after life. We both wanted to learn more.

"Look at this!" said Herman. "Rabbi Spitz studied with Dr. Brian Weiss. He's a psychiatrist who claims that he hypnotizes people all the way back to past lives."

"Yes, I know about his work. I've read several of his books. Dr. Weiss has impressive credentials. He was a graduate of Yale Medical School and chairman of the Department of Psychiatry at Mt. Sinai Hospital in Miami."

I explained that Dr. Weiss regresses his patients to help them discover traumas in their former lives that may have a lingering influence on the present. Sometimes they're able to release the physical and emotional pain of the past and become well.

"Yes," responded Herman. "Dr. Weiss also believes that we travel in soul groups and reconnect with the same people over the course of many lives. We may come back as a different sex, religion, or race, but the same souls reunite as family and friends to help each other learn and grow."

"Do you think that's possible, Dad?"

He chuckled. "Mom and I used to joke that we felt as though we were together before, that this wasn't the first time. But if it's true that we are reborn, maybe I won't see Mom after I die. Maybe she won't wait for me."

"Oh, Dad. Mom would wait forever."

"I hope so," he said, a slight smile playing on his lips.

"And," he added, "do you suppose you could bring me Dr. Weiss's books? I want to learn more."

RABBI SPITZ PROVIDED DETAILS on the research of near-death experience. Drs. Raymond Moody and Elizabeth Kubler-Ross interviewed thousands of patients who had died and were revived. Upon their death many reported drifting upward toward the ceiling in a body that was weightless and whole. They watched the resuscitation from above, and their vision became hyper-acute, allowing them to see through walls. Blind patients were able to describe the clothing of physicians and the instruments that were used. Although they heard and understood what was being said, when they tried to speak with the doctors or nurses, no one heard them. It was then that they realized that they were dead.

Many described the tunnel and emergence into a warm and embracing light. In the light they were welcomed by relatives who were in the prime of life despite being ill or elderly when they died. Thoughts were shared. No words were spoken. Souls recognized souls.

Next came a life review. It was a panorama of their own lives and their impact on the lives they touched. The love, the anger, the joy, the hurt that they caused was personally and powerfully experienced. There is no outside judgment. We judge ourselves. There is no pain, only peace.

When people were resuscitated, they found the brilliance and the beauty of the next realm impossible to describe. Each survivor returned with a new view of death—and of life. Fear dissolved, making room for awareness, appreciation, and awe.

As Herman read on he was stunned to learn that Judaism, in both the Talmud and the mystical writings of the Zohar, made reference to acceptance of mediumship—communication with deceased souls. Rabbi Spitz explained that some Jewish sages were believed to have had the ability to see the past lives of their followers and to receive messages from departed souls. According to the Talmud, Jewish law does allow one to consult a medium that is "simply telling you what he or she is hearing." What is not allowed, however, explains Rabbi Spitz, is the idolatry of calling the souls through incantations, specific clothing, or incense. Use of mediums to forecast the future is also forbidden.

Does the Soul Survive? introduced Herman to the work of the well-known mediums James Van Praagh and George Anderson. He asked me to bring him their writings. Their books explain that death is not the end of the soul's existence and that connection with loved ones who have passed can comfort, support, and enrich our lives.

Herman began to read extensively about past lives, near-death experiences, and ultimate reconnection with loved ones and with God. His exploration gave him hope that Betty was safe, that her soul survived, and that one day they might be together again.

SOON AFTER my father and I learned of the acceptance of spirit communication by some Jewish scholars, I received a surprising phone call. My friends Dot and Trish had a message for me—a message they said was from my mother. Dot and Trish, women who had adopted both of my parents as their own, were members of a Spiritualist church in Boston.

"Michele, it's been nine months since your mother passed away, and she wants to talk to you!"

"What do you mean, she wants to talk to me?" I asked in amazement.

"When we went to church this morning, Betty came to us. She's fine, and she wants you to know that. We signed you up for a reading with our minister. It's for next Friday."

I was both stunned and curious. With trepidation I agreed to keep the appointment, yet I told no one that I was going. I was certain they'd question my sanity. I did.

THURSDAY NIGHT I couldn't sleep. It was one thing to read about mediums, but consulting one to get a message from my mother frightened me. How would I know if it were she? I was going alone—what if the church was haunted? What if the minister was a charlatan? What on Earth was I doing?

After a long subway ride and a several-block walk, I found the church. It was a neat, well-kept building on a beautiful tree-lined street. My body shook as I rang the bell.

"Hello, welcome," said a tall, handsome, dark-haired man with a radiant smile. "Please come in. I'm Reverend Matthew." He extended his hand to me. "I'll be right with you. Please have a seat."

Moments later the minister, smiling gently, sat across from me and turned on the tape recorder. My heart pounded so that I wondered if that, too, would be recorded.

"A woman comes to me. There is a family resemblance, but she shows herself to be heavier and taller than you. She is walking with a jaunty stride. This same woman came earlier, before you arrived, and I asked her to return when it was time to meet her loved one. They occasionally do that when they are especially eager to connect. Is it your mother who is in spirit? Please just answer yes or no."

I shook my head yes, still too nervous to talk. Earlier that morning I prayed for my mother to meet me at the church. Evidently she got there before I did! Of one thing I was certain—my friends assured me that they gave Reverend Matthew no information about why I was coming nor whom I lost.

"Your mother wants you to know that she is well and moving easily. That's why she showed herself with a bouncy walk. She was a Renaissance Woman, very intelligent and creative. She had a quick wit, a delightful sense of humor, and she was incredibly loving. But she never hesitated to speak her mind. She tells you that you need to be more like that. Your mother shows me a brilliant nature scene, and now she's put a frame around it. I don't believe that she was a painter—rather that she appreciated art and taught you to love it as well. She looks at you with deep love and appreciation. I see that although you were mother and daughter, you were more like sisters. She says thank you for supporting her always and for your devotion until the end.

"Now she is showing me her husband. He is a strikingly handsome man. She's telling me something intimate—that she fell in love with him the first time they met. Your mother says that their marriage was very loving, but that there was some conflict at the end. They need to talk when it is his time. And when it is his time, she and his mother will be waiting for him. They are praying for him now."

I was beginning to relax by the time the reverend asked if I had any questions. "Yes—what is my mother doing now?"

"She says she's traveling, visiting all of the places she and your father loved. Only she says that she doesn't need a ticket. All she has to do is snap her fingers and she's there. Your mother wants you to know that she's happy, healthy, and peaceful, and that she is waiting for your father."

I LEFT THE CHURCH feeling that my mother had come to me. The details offered were specific and unknown to anyone else. I was incredibly grateful and relieved. What if I were to tell my father? Would he be as elated as I? After all, now he understood that mediumship, if done properly, wasn't considered heresy.

I went directly to the Shalom Center.

"Dad, I have something to tell you. I am just back from a visit to Dot and Trish's church. I met with their minister, who's a medium like James Van Praagh and George Anderson. Dad, he gave me messages from Mom."

Herman sat forward in his chair, his eyes opened wide. "Tell me, what did he say?"

"He said that Mom is well and happy and that she's traveling!"

"Traveling?"

"Yes, Dad. And Mom said that she doesn't need a ticket. She just snaps her fingers and she's there. She's going to all of the places you loved to visit."

"That sounds like my sweetheart!" Herman said with tears in his eyes. "And she's well?"

"Yes, Dad. Mom told the reverend she's fine, and she's walking with a spring in her step. She said that she loves us."

We held each other and cried.

BORN KNOWING

STUDYING HEBREW, ATTENDING SERVICES, AND learning more of Jewish history and tradition stirred a yearning in me. For many years I had practiced a form of Buddhist meditation, belonged to a women's inter-faith spirituality group, and attended monthly Sufi gatherings learning about Islamic mysticism. I began to wonder, is it possible that Judaism, my own faith, offers the rich spirituality my soul was seeking?

Perhaps it was time to join a synagogue and connect with a rabbi who could be my teacher and guide. I had heard of a woman rabbi in the next town whose services were filled with song and joy. At the end of the summer of 2003 I met Rabbi Ilana Rosansky at the Temple's open house. I listened enthralled as the rabbi related stories of Jewish mysticism and Kabbalah. Yes, it was time for me to explore my own faith, and the time was now.

How, though, would Herman feel about a female rabbi? He grew up in the Orthodox tradition, where women and men were not allowed to sit together in services, nor were women permitted to read from the Torah. They were not even counted as part of the *minyan*, the quorum of ten needed to say the holiest of prayers. Certainly there were no Orthodox women rabbis. And yet, I wanted my father to know.

"Dad, I have something to tell you."

"Yes?"

"David and I joined a synagogue."

"How wonderful! That makes me very happy."

"Dad, there's more."

"What is it?"

"The rabbi is a woman."

My father paused and glanced upward. Slowly, very slowly, he answered. "Well, she's a person."

Herman never, ever, spoke ill of anyone. He certainly wasn't going to start with a rabbi—even if it did seem that the world was being turned upside down.

"Dad, would you like to meet Rabbi Rosansky?"

"Very much. I want to thank her."

RABBI ROSANSKY and Herman Liss were drawn to each other like magnets. If at first Herman couldn't fathom the concept of a female rabbi, he soon became an ardent supporter.

There were former congregants who now lived at the Shalom Center. The rabbi would visit with them and would then come to my father's room. Together they explored questions of ethics and edicts and soul. At times their conversations were light and playful and other times probing and deliberate. The rabbi often stayed twice as long as she had intended because of their growing affinity.

After their visit, I'd often receive a call. "Michele, your father makes me feel at home. He asks a lot of thoughtful questions with such warmth and good humor. I usually save his visit for last, sort of like dessert—like good chocolate, to be savored."

Another time the rabbi told me, "Today I could tell that Herman wasn't feeling well. But it's amazing. Even when he's having a bad day, it's a good day. He has a gift for making other people feel good, no matter what *he* might be feeling."

Late one evening I received a call from Rabbi Rosansky. "I've had a long, challenging day," she said, "and your father was the highlight."

"He was?"

"Yes, I came into his room totally spent—maybe looking for a little comfort myself. You know, there are a few rare people, beacons of how God wishes us all to be with each other. That's Herman. He's a reminder of how God intends man to be on this Earth. Do you know what I mean?"

I knew exactly what she meant.

My own fascination with Jewish mysticism had grown under Rabbi Rosansky's tutelage. She taught a class on Kabbalah, and as I learned I shared my unfolding awareness with my father. Each afternoon he and I read together from texts and articles that explored man's connection to God. We learned that our acts of lovingkindness bring us closer to the Divine. Kabbalah teaches that through study and prayer, intention and contemplation, love and compassion, and good deeds, our spirits unite with God. In reflecting God's own goodness, we repair our souls and those of others. We help to heal the world—*Tikkun Olam.*

"Why didn't I know this?" my father lamented. "Why am I just learning this now?"

"Dad, you were born knowing this! You've lived it your entire life."

In Kabbalah it is said that when God created the world, he contracted his Infinite Self to provide space for creation. After my mother's passing and Herman's recovery, I realized that my father had contracted his own self to allow for my mother's fullest light. Herman was Betty's finest audience. When she was alive he stayed in the background, encouraging her to be front and center. He listened delightedly as she told her stories. He smiled and laughed, content just to be with her, to give her the limelight. He was happiest when she shone.

After Betty died, my friends and family noticed a fascinating change in Herman. He was a man who was more than sweet and kind and gentle. He was brilliant and articulate and strong. Herman's own humor and insight and sharp intelligence became evident, one conversation after another.

Like God, Herman, out of his infinite love, had contracted himself to let Betty shine. Herman brought heaven down to Earth.

CARD GAMES
MICHAEL

ONE RAINY VACATION DAY, MY MOM PLANNED FOR me to meet with Herman for the entire morning. Most of the time I spent only an hour with Herman once a week. The sky outside was dark and almost foreboding, but the atmosphere inside the nursing home was pleasant and safe.

It had been an ancient stereotype of mine that people in nursing homes love to play cards and bingo, and knit. So I brought a deck of cards for Herman and asked him if he knew any games.

"I was never very big into card games," he said. "Something about them never appealed to me. If you want to play cards, we will."

I'm screwed, I thought. Well, I never really enjoyed cards, either. Everyone in my family loves cards, especially my mom, and they devise all sorts of strategies and nuances in their games that I just never want to be a part of.

"Well, I know a game," I said. My mom had showed me a game the day before that I had moderately enjoyed. I thought I knew the rules, but it turns out I was very shaky on them when she wasn't there.

"Well, I think you start off by putting a card in the pile. Now you take a card that's bigger than that—or no, maybe it's less. I have to start over. I messed it all up."

Herman listened patiently. We played a pathetic little game that didn't really have any rules in it. It had some substance, but the rules were forever changing, and nobody ended up winning. Herman thought this was very funny, but was too polite to say anything. Eventually we reached a silent agreement to stop playing cards.

We went back into Herman's room, and he did something he was good at—he told me a long, interesting, and funny story that took up the rest of the morning.

FRIENDS WHO BECAME FAMILY

As Herman's wisdom and spirit expanded, so too did his family. People of all faiths, colors, cultures, and nationalities were drawn to him. "I love him like a father," was repeated to me with Spanish, Indian, African, Asian, Russian, and American inflections.

My dear friend Chang-Chen Chen, born and raised in Taiwan, had lived in the United States only briefly when she met Herman. Chang-Chen moved to Massachusetts with her teenage sons to give them the opportunity to study in this country.

Chang-Chen and her boys called Herman "Uncle," the Chinese expression of respect for an older man. Herman introduced them as his niece and nephews. But Chang-Chen and Herman were closer than niece and uncle. They were kindred souls. They explored the essence of their faiths. He taught her about Judaism, and she taught him about Buddhism.

My father asked me, "Do you know how much Judaism and Buddhism share? The ethics are the same. In our faith we're taught to do justice, to be kind and humble, to open our doors to strangers, and to pursue peace. Chang-Chen tells me that Buddhism teaches the same things—kindness, compassion, goodness, and caring.

"I want to learn more," he told me. "Please, bring me books about Buddhism."

Herman read works by the Dalai Lama and Ram Dass and Jon Kabat-Zinn. He told me, "At heart all people are the same. We're all connected. We're all one."

Chang-Chen and Herman's closeness bolstered them both in their new lives. When she contemplated applying for her first job in this country, she shyly expressed her reservations to Herman. Chang-Chen, who in her own country had been an accountant and department supervisor of an international firm, was feeling unsure.

"I'm thinking of working in a bank, but my English is still poor. I don't know if people will understand me. Maybe I won't pass the tests. But my older son is leaving for college, and the younger is going to boarding school. I really want to help support them and my parents back home."

Herman encouraged Chang-Chen. "You can do this. You're smart, and people will be drawn to you. Have confidence in yourself. I believe in you. This will be the beginning of a wonderful new life. Auntie Betty would be so proud."

Chang-Chen applied and was accepted for an entry-level teller position. Her developing English did not hold her back. Within months Chang-Chen was recognized as the top account salesperson in her bank's region. As Herman had predicted, she was promoted and moved to a busier branch.

"Congratulations, Chang-Chen," Herman beamed when he learned of her success. He kissed her hands. "They're so lucky to have you!"

Chang-Chen visited Herman nearly every weekend, and if I had to be away she'd come after work to check on him. One Sunday while I was out of town, Chang-Chen became concerned about Herman's watery and itchy eyes. She asked the nurse on duty if she had something to relieve the tearing and burning.

"Excuse me," Chang-Chen said to a nurse she had not met before. "Mr. Liss's eyes are hurting him."

The nurse ignored her.

Chang-Chen tried again. "How do you do. My name is Chang-Chen, and I'm here visiting Herman Liss. He needs some help."

Again she was ignored.

Thinking that it might show respect to address the nurse personally, she asked, "Please tell me your name."

"Why do want to know that?" responded the woman defensively.

Chang-Chen returned to the room concerned. "Uncle, is the nurse on duty rude to you?"

"Oh, I know who you mean. She's usually here on weekend evenings. That's just the way she is. My own nurse will be back tomorrow, and she'll know what to give me. Don't worry."

Two weeks after Chang-Chen's encounter with this night nurse, the nurse was dismissed. Her replacement was a warm, wonderful Kenyan whose laugh echoed up and down the hall. The new nurse told me, "Your father reminds me so much of my own Dad, who is on the other side of the world. I really miss him. Do you think Herman would mind if I adopt him as my American Dad?"

"No," I laughed. "But you're sure going to have a lot of siblings!"

ONE SPRING SUNDAY when Chang-Chen came to visit, Herman was reading the sports section of the *Boston Globe*. He spoke at length about the new Red Sox management and their emphasis on team unity and brotherhood.

"The game is going to be on TV in a few minutes. Would you like to watch it with me?" Chang-Chen asked.

"Do you like baseball?" Herman replied.

Chang-Chen, supposing that Herman adored sports, answered enthusiastically, "Yes, Uncle."

Truthfully, Chang-Chen's younger son was an avid fan, and when baseball was on she'd leave the room. Herman, thinking that Chang-Chen wanted to see the game, tried to appear equally enthused. In the 28 years I knew him, never did he watch baseball. He merely read the sports page, just as he read every other page in the paper. And yet, from that afternoon on, each Sunday Chang-Chen would come just in time for the start of the game. They sat side by side, cheering the Red Sox, neither knowing the other's secret. Their yelps and hollers became as real and fervent as if they'd always been ardent fans.

Chang-Chen told me, "We have a Chinese saying, 'Giving love is always greater than to be loved.' I really didn't understand it until I met Uncle Herman. I've never met anyone like him before. I'd like to give him a spirit award. He's a model for every age."

THERE ARE NO WORDS

IT WASN'T JUST WOMEN WHO ADOPTED HERMAN AS their own. Men, too, met him and fell in love. Sidney, a widower in his early eighties, was a weekly volunteer at the Shalom Center. Herman and Sidney had attended a luncheon outing where they sat across from one another. Mesmerized by Herman, Sidney began visiting his new friend each Thursday morning. They'd discuss world events, history, books, and their personal lives. After every visit Sidney would present Herman with the latest copy of *Newsweek,* and Herman would say, "Thank you, Sidney. When I finish reading it I'll pass it on to Ike. He appreciates the magazines, too."

Often I'd arrive toward the end of Sidney's visits, just before lunch. Together we'd wheel my Dad, now unable to walk, into the dining room. Once Herman was settled, Sidney and I would go into the lounge to talk.

"Michele," he told me, "I volunteer at the Shalom Center to help the elderly. My mother used to live here, so I feel an attachment to the place. But meeting with Herman lifts *me,* makes *me* feel good. He gives *me* hope. To see a man of his age, after losing his wife and suffering a stroke, cope as he does—well, it inspires me. He's still vibrant and well-spoken. I never think of him as a particular age."

"Sidney, my father speaks of you a lot. He loves hearing about your adventures as a jeweler and about your travels to Europe to buy stones. I thank you for being so devoted to him."

"Really, I benefit more than he does. I'm very lonely since losing my wife. It's so hard. When I see Herman I can be honest with him. He's interested in my experience and my troubles. He really cares. He listens. I can tell him anything. He understands. He's concerned. Imagine that!"

"I know. I feel so lucky that he came into my mother's life and mine."

"What do you mean, 'came into your life?'"

"I thought Herman told you. I was an adult when he married my mother."

"No, but he talks about you all the time. I've never seen such love between a father and a daughter. I'm very surprised to learn that he didn't raise you!"

"Actually, I never think about Herman being my stepfather. I couldn't love him more if I were born to him."

Sidney went on. "I know what you're saying. He's unlike anyone I've ever met. I watch as people who barely speak English come into his room to clean. He thanks them, gives them such respect. Everyone is special to Herman. They hug him, smile at him, and answer him in their own language. The words don't matter. They understand each other. I've never seen anything like it."

"People are drawn to him. I see this, too," I agreed.

"I've been all over the world in my work," Sidney continued, "but never before met a man like Herman. I have a special kind of love for him. He's changed my life."

FOUR LEGGED LOVE

ONE OF HERMAN'S FAVORITE VISITORS WAS A FOUR-legged guest named Snoopy, a cairn terrier with Benji eyes. Snoopy never stopped. He raced, he leapt, he stalked squirrels and chased blowing leaves. Snoopy took juicy bites out of life.

"What would you think about bringing Snoopy to visit Dad the next time you come?" I asked Snoopy's parents and my close friends, Hedy and Sal Lopes. "He loves animals, and lots of people bring their dogs to the Shalom Center."

"That would be risky," Hedy laughed. "You know he gets easily excited. A ball of dust sets him off."

"If he gets out of control, I'll take him outside while you and Sal visit. I just think that Dad would love to see him. His nurse Lori brings in her pit bull pups for him to play with, and he raves about them. He's even put their pictures up on his bulletin board. Let's just try."

The next Sunday Snoopy trotted into the Shalom Center. He was dressed in a tiny skullcap and prayer shawl, miniature versions of the ones my father wore in the synagogue. When he saw Herman, he bounded over to the wheelchair and sat quietly staring up at him.

"Look at this," chuckled Herman. "In your yarmulke and tallis, you look like a little Jewish dog."

Sal lifted Snoopy onto my father's lap. Snoopy licked Herman's face and then sat relaxed as Herman petted him.

"Let's take him for a walk," Herman suggested, "so the other people can enjoy Snoopy, too."

We wheeled Dad and Snoopy into the residents' lounge. Herman asked to be taken to each person so they could pet Snoopy. The men and women—some of whom barely responded to me in the past—came alive as they patted and cooed to Snoopy.

Snoopy neither barked nor wriggled as they rubbed his fur and kissed his face and paws. He and Herman were a rolling therapy team.

THE HEARING HEART

"**L**ORI, I CAN SEE THAT YOU'RE NOT OK TO-day," Herman said. "You haven't been yourself for quite a while. You look sad, and I'm worried about you. Is there anything I can do to help?"

Lori began to cry, quietly at first, and then from her depths. "Herman, I'm so unhappy. I've been in a relationship now for several years, but I'm terribly unhappy. There is no respect, no appreciation, just pain. I don't know what to do or how to get out of it."

"I see that the spark has gone out of your eyes, and your laughter—well, that's gone, too."

"I can't continue. It hurts so bad."

"Please, don't allow anyone, especially someone you gave your heart to, to treat you badly. You're gentle, you're thoughtful, you care so much about all of us—please care about yourself."

"Herman, when I hear you talk about your wife, I know how much you loved her, and still love her. Your stories melt my heart. It makes me wonder if I could ever have a marriage like that—kind and loving, full of devotion."

"That's what you deserve, Lori. You must believe this."

"I'm feeling so confused. It feels like I'm in a prison, and I'm suffocating."

"Lori, you're young. You have so much love to share. You can't allow yourself to serve a life sentence. Please think about yourself and your future. How do you want to live?"

"Herman, what I want most of all is to find a man just like you."

HERMAN & OTHERS

MICHAEL

HERMAN HAD AN UNWAVERING CONCERN FOR OTH-
ers. He asked, "Is there anything I can do to help?" almost
every time I visited. And his belief "Treat the next fellow as
you'd want to be treated" wasn't just words. He lived it.

After all, he invited me to work with him on making a giant card
and poster for his friend Chang-Chen, who had just been promoted
at her job at a bank. He signed the card, cut out flowers, decorated
a border, and proudly displayed the bank's logo. Herman spent time
helping people. Most people, if they did anything, would run out and
sign their name on a Hallmark card.

Herman seemed to grow as I grew. He enjoyed watching me become
mature, and felt as though my accomplishments were his accomplishments. At our picnic in July 2003 I took my piano book over to Herman and played him tunes. He began to clap, and it seemed to me that
because I had played those songs Herman felt almost as though he had
played those songs. I showed Herman some cartoons I had drawn, and
Herman began to ask me about my future—making colorful suggestions.

When my dad was laid off from work, Herman made suggestions
about what my dad could do. He wanted to think there was some way
he could help him. He suggested my dad hone his talents as a filmmaker and film people's weddings, anniversaries, bar/bat mitzvahs, etc.
He suggested I become a cartoonist, and told me that I have such talent
that I could do whatever I wanted.

That was one of Herman's purposes in life—others.

I felt lucky to know such a kind man. I felt I could say or ask anything of him because he was so good-natured. I felt like Herman was my grandfather. Maybe it was because he cared so much.

STILL GROWING

AT NEARLY NINETY-FOUR NOT ONLY WAS HERMAN alive, he thrived. Herman's world steadily expanded. Each morning after breakfast he returned to his room to read the newspaper that he then delivered to his good friend Ike. At lunch they'd discuss the articles. Their combined one-hundred-and-eighty-eight years provided a perspective that deepened their understanding of the issues. They'd share recollections and insights gleaned from their tapestry of experiences as sons and fathers, students and teachers, citizens and soldiers, youths and elders.

Reading became Herman's passion. I made frequent trips to the library to select books that would captivate him, and they weren't hard to find. History, biographies, business, politics, sports, the entertainment industry, and humor were among his requests. As I returned to the Shalom Center with stack after stack of books, the staff would ask to see the titles. Invariably they'd comment, "Your father is the best-read person in the Shalom Center, and that includes us!"

Herman's growing fascination was comparative religion—particularly the mystical links between the faiths.

"You know," posited Herman after completing a book on Islam, "the Koran teaches peace. The Koran and the Bible both instill a reverence for God. Most people—Muslims, Jews, Buddhists, Christians, Hindus, whatever their faith—want to live in harmony. We are all connected, aren't we? Abraham was the father of Judaism, Christianity, and Islam. Why do people fight and kill each other? War is a nightmare and not the way to solve problems. This isn't what God asks of us. We are all His children, and he loves us all the same."

Herman stopped and thought for a moment. "Look at the Shalom Center. It's a melting pot. We're from all over the globe, and we get along. We learn from each other and celebrate the holidays together. Really, our differences don't have to divide us."

THE SHALOM CENTER was a community of compassion that honored the total wellbeing of their residents. Each week musicians and singers came to entertain, and the staff sang and danced with the audience. Familiar melodies evoked deep memories of vibrance and youth and delight. Jazz, tunes from World War II, and lively ethnic songs touched the souls of people whose minds and bodies appeared frozen—yet the music stirred them. Those who could no longer speak or who wandered aimlessly sang and swayed and came alive.

Classes from local schools came to entertain and visit as well. Together with the elders they painted, created pottery, and baked. Recent movies were shown in the center's theater, and classic movies played in the lounges. Herman delighted in the trips outside the facility, when he and his friends were taken to restaurants, concerts, and plays. It was my special joy to accompany these eager travelers as a chaperone.

One of the special highlights for me was a trip with my father to Boston Symphony Hall to hear Keith Lockhart conduct the Boston Pops. It was Herman's first experience at a Pops concert, and he relished every note. At the end of the program a Shalom Center administrator asked Herman if she could take him upstairs for a photo with Mr. Lockhart. As the world-renowned conductor approached my father, Herman held out his hand and said, "Thank you for a spectacular afternoon. Thank you for sharing your gift!"

The flash popped and the photographer captured the conductor and Herman in profile, mutual appreciation in their gaze. The picture appeared on the cover of the Shalom Center publication *Generations*. The page was awash in light.

THE EMBRACE

ERMAN'S MIND AND HEART FLOURISHED, YET HIS body weakened. Nurses, aides, and doctors attended to him not as just a patient, but as a beloved parent or friend. Maria, his assistant, cared for his most intimate needs. She bathed him, dressed him, and made certain he was comfortable.

"Herman, would you like a bath or a shower today?" she would ask.

"A bath, please," was his usual reply. "It relaxes me. I've never had bubble baths before."

"It's a special tub, Herman. The air bubbles massage your muscles, and that's what feels so good on your sore back and knees. Why don't you spend some extra time in there and really relax?"

"Thank you, Maria. Thank you so much. You're so good to me."

Each evening Herman and Maria talked as she readied him for bed. Maria remembered her life in Colombia as one of eight children. Herman told stories about his own life. Mostly they talked about family.

"Herman, my parents and brothers and sisters are still in Colombia. My husband and I are here with our two boys. I'd like them to meet you, if it's OK."

"Oh, that would be wonderful. Please bring them. How old are they?"

"The little one is six and the older one is eleven."

"What do they like to do?"

"Jose, the older boy, is an athlete, and he loves to dance. Pedro likes to draw. He's very imaginative. I'll bring them next week, Herman."

HERMAN AND JOSE AND PEDRO made a fast connection. The boys brought cards that they designed, and immediately Herman hung them on his wall. He asked the children about their school, their friends, and their hobbies. Jose and Pedro asked their mother if they could return. Herman made them feel special—and there was something else. They loved his birdfeeder.

When Herman was first transferred to Maria's side of the hall, she suggested that I get him a birdfeeder to hang on the outside of his picture window. "There's a tree right in front of his room, and it attracts lots of songbirds. I bet he'll enjoy seeing them so close."

Within days goldfinches, chickadees, cardinals, sparrows, and wrens found the feeder. Herman watched gleefully as they chased each other, cracked the seeds, and flew to and from the tree.

"Look, the cardinals are back—*shhh.* Let's watch them," he'd say, stopping conversation.

The birds drew staff and other residents to Herman's room to enjoy the show. They'd leave smiling and relaxed, particularly when the scarlet flyers came to feed.

A FEW WEEKS after Herman met Jose and Pedro, the Guadalupe family grew. A cousin from Florida moved into their home with her two boys. The seven-year-old had been born with severe handicaps and was unable to walk or speak. Swallowing had become increasingly difficult, and he was rapidly losing weight.

Soon Maria brought all four boys to visit Herman. Dad asked if the little one could be lifted onto his lap. He held him like a baby, and they gazed into each other's eyes and smiled.

That afternoon my father asked me, "Michele, is there any way we can help this child? He's so ill. He has no strength. He's like a tiny bird."

"Dad, I know Maria is trying to make an appointment for him to see a doctor. He'll need a specialist. His case is very complicated."

"You know that can take a long time. This family can't wait. Don't you know someone who can help?"

Help? I thought. Where would I find help? Then I remembered. "I'm not sure, Dad, but I do have a friend who's a physician in Boston who works with profoundly disabled children. I'll call her and see what she suggests."

"Please! This family needs help now. They need a miracle! God willing, this will make a difference."

I spoke to my friend that evening and told her about this precious boy and my father's fervent prayers. She immediately called the family and spoke to them in fluent Spanish, making an appointment to see the child the next day. Soon after his examination, a team of highly skilled surgeons performed a life-saving operation and inserted a feeding tube.

Within days the fragile little boy began gaining weight. His strength increased, and with therapy and time he was able to push his walker into my father's room. Together they sat, side by side, holding hands, watching the birds and laughing.

STRUGGLE & STRENGTH

SHORTLY AFTER HERMAN'S NINETY-FOURTH BIRTH-day I received an early morning call from Lori. "Michele, your father is having difficulty. His blood pressure is up. We've increased his medication, but the pressure continues to rise. Herman's also having more problems breathing. His congestive heart failure seems to be worsening. When I came in to check him this morning, he told me something I think you should know."

"Yes, Lori?"

"Herman said that your mother and his came to him last night, and they're getting ready for him to join them. Michele, it's different than the last time when he talked about dying. Then he asked us to help him die. Now, he's not depressed. He's very calm, totally peaceful."

"Do you think he needs someone to talk to—maybe a psychologist or rabbi?"

"Honestly, Michele, I think it's time to consider hospice support. We have a number of residents who are seen by hospice right here at the Shalom Center. They have a chaplain, a social worker, and skilled nurses and aides who provide additional care that could be important for your dad."

"I don't think my father is near death. Do you?"

"Not right away, but I think Herman should be evaluated by hospice to see if he qualifies for their services. He has multiple physical problems, and given his age and uncontrolled symptoms, I think it's important."

Lori continued, "I'm concerned about him because Herman never asks for anything. He never wants to bother anyone. Last month, in all that heat, he had to be hospitalized for dehydration. He must have been thirsty and uncomfortable, but he didn't ask for water. If hospice is involved there can be another pair of eyes and hands. And his sense that his family is coming to him—well, sometimes that's a sign to be taken seriously."

"Lori, I know you're right about involving hospice. My concern is that my father thinks of it as a sign of lost hope. When I requested hospice for my mother, Herman felt that I called in the Angels of Death."

"Yes, unfortunately hospice is often called toward the very end. But it doesn't have to be that way. Hospice is about enriching the quality of life and giving the patients and their families compassionate, gentle, loving care. They also have a palliative care program for people who have progressive illnesses and are in pain but are not ready for full hospice support. Herman could benefit from that tremendously. And when the staff meets Herman, it will be a gift for everyone."

"OK, Lori, but first I have to figure out how to tell him."

"Sure. Whenever you're ready, Michele."

I NEEDED help. I felt as though I was yanked back to the previous summer when my mother fell ill. The shadowed triplets—Panic, Confusion, and Dread—re-emerged.

When Mom was failing I had discovered a secluded nook by the edge of the sea, a peace hollow. There, on a craggy boulder jutting up from the tides, was a cradle just large enough to hold me. On this day I walked the two miles to Castle Rock on Marblehead Neck, climbed up to my comfort space and melted in. Blue touching blue.

"Please," I prayed to God—to my mother—to the universe—to anyone out there. "What should I do? What should I say?"

I waited. Warmed by the sun and heated rock, lulled by the lapping waves, I drifted, then heard, "Tell him that *you* need help."

"Tell him *I* need help?"

"Don't you?"

"Yes, of course I do."

"Then just listen! Tell Herman that soon it will be a year since your mother's funeral. Tell him that you will all be going to the grave for the first time, for the unveiling of the headstone. Tell him that you're struggling. And most important, tell him that hospice can help *you*."

"Tell him that hospice can help *me*?"

"That's right. Explain that since your mom was a hospice patient, you as a family member qualify for grief counseling."

"You want me to tell my father that we should connect with hospice because *I'm* in pain?"

"You got it! You know Herman would do anything to help you."

"Yes, that's true."

"Well, he'll be doing this for you, and in the meantime Herman will receive the services he needs as well. It's perfect!"

Was this voice coming from inside my own head or from a loving source? I guessed it really didn't matter, as long as it would help.

That afternoon I spoke to Herman in his room. "Dad, I have a huge favor to ask you."

"Yes, what can I do?"

"I'm having a problem. Soon it will be the first anniversary of Mom's passing, and I'm having a hard time. I don't think I've fully mourned."

"I know what you mean. How can I help?"

"Dad, hospice has been checking with me to see how we're doing since Mom died. They told me that as family members of one of their patients, we qualify for grief counseling. I think it could help me. But we're a team, Dad, you and I, and I'd like you to do this with me. Please!"

"If it's going to help you, sweetheart, then go ahead and call hospice."

"Thanks. You don't know how much I appreciate this."

I left to speak with Lori. "Please call hospice for us. My father agreed, but he will not be thinking of himself as a hospice patient—just as a support for me. Please let them know that."

"That sounds like Herman! He's still trying to take care of you."

Hospice became a gift for us all. Lori was right. Over the months the nurses and chaplains, the social worker, volunteers, and aides became a precious support for my father and myself. Hospice helped to stabilize Herman, and he began to feel stronger than he had in a long while. So did I.

Amazed and grateful for my father's improvement, I repeatedly thanked the hospice staff.

"You don't know, Michele, what Herman has done for me," said one hospice worker after another.

I received frequent calls and notes and hugs of gratitude. Each, in personal expression, shared similar thoughts. "Herman encourages. Herman listens. Herman cares. Herman teaches. Herman understands. Herman forgives. Herman loves. Herman is a Holy Man."

HALLOWEEN

IN THE AUTUMN OF 2003, NEARLY A YEAR AFTER HERman moved to the Shalom Center, the Halloween excitement began to build. Herman was amused to be going as a lady of the evening, just as Betty had wished. For weeks I had been searching for a seductive outfit that would fit his six-foot two-hundred-and-ten-pound frame. Each time I found something promising, I'd bring it to Dad for a fitting and approval.

The first item I discovered was a flame-red stretch tube top.

Dad burst with laughter. "Can I fill this out so I look really sexy?"

"Oh, yeah," I said as I reached for his gym socks.

Now I began my hunt for short shorts that would coordinate with the skimpy top. But the women's departments had nothing alluring in his size. Then it struck me. What if I could find a pair of men's silky boxer shorts?

Success! I discovered a pair of black extra-large nylon boxers covered with red and green hot chili peppers. Perfect!

"This is wonderful," Herman laughed as he looked at his evolving costume. "Now do you think you could find me a flashing light to tape over my navel? It would glow right through my shorts."

I had no idea how to find that specialty item, but I promised I'd try. I was in a drugstore when I unexpectedly found the answer. A pulsating spark attached to my father's brand of joint relief supplement caught my eye. There it was, our flashing red navel light!

We decided that Herman's hair should be blonde and flowing. I dug out the wig from the bathing beauty and angel eras. For his feet I found a delicate pair of size-twelve red, green and gold Chinese slippers.

"Uh, this is very nice of you, Michele—but if it wouldn't be too much trouble, I'd prefer a pair of heels, really high!"

How was I going to pull this one off? But he wanted those shoes so badly that I began to search. Still, I couldn't imagine Herman squeezing his enormous feet—now swollen—into a pair of high heels. And where on Earth would I find them?

I combed through countless racks of shoes in endless stores. Nothing! But one day, on a whim, I stopped at a discount shoe store that advertised a sale on hard-to-find sizes. There, near the bottom of a tall bin, I pulled out an enormous pair of sling-back black velvet open-toed shoes with three-inch heels.

This was it! Dad's toes could overlap in the front with the heels spilling over the back. I could snip the dainty straps and extend them with black electrical tape if necessary. Since he'd be in his wheelchair, it didn't matter that they weren't functional.

ON OCTOBER 30, the day of the Halloween party, only Dad, Lori, Maria, and I knew of the plan. The parade and judging were to start at two o'clock. Maria came to his room before one o'clock for the shower and shave and moustache trim. As she and Lori got him into his costume, I dressed Herman's wheelchair in orange and yellow crepe paper, weaving it through the spokes. On the back of the chair I hung the sign that Dad designed. It read, "Tons of Fun—only $2 dollars plus 5% entertainment tax."

When Maria and Lori brought Herman out of the bathroom, we were all howling. He got settled in his chair and on went the wig and in went the stuffing. What a babe!

Maria, holding his high heels, asked, "Where are his stockings?"

"Stockings? What do you mean, stockings?" I asked, puzzled.

"Michele, we have a few minutes left. While we put on his makeup, run down to the pharmacy. They have queen-size fishnet thigh-highs. Find the largest size they have. They'll fit. By the way, pick up a pair of false eyelashes while you're there!"

I raced the three blocks to the drugstore, found the stocking display and the super-size thigh highs. I charged to the counter, aware that in minutes Herman would have to be ready for the parade.

The gray haired cashier took a look at my flushed face, fishnet stockings, and false eyelashes and gave me a strange look.

"No," I laughed. "They're not mine! They're for my father."

She rolled her eyes.

"Really, my father is ninety-four, and he lives at the Shalom Center. He's dressing as a hooker for Halloween!"

"This I'd like to see!"

I sprinted back with just minutes to spare before the parade. Maria pulled on the stockings and applied his eyelashes. Herman's lipstick, eye shadow, and blush completed the look. Lori—dressed in her cousin's suit, fedora hat, and gold chains with a money sign—gave Dad a kiss for luck. She pushed him down the hall to the elevator.

When the doors opened to the first floor lobby, residents and visitors took a look at the flaxen-haired hooker and began to scream. The shouts, stomping, and laughter were deafening.

Herman smiled, waved, and blew kisses. Lori wheeled him to the front of the line to lead the parade. Herman, by a show of applause, won first prize.

I stood several feet away taking pictures. An elderly woman, a visitor, asked in a smug voice, "Who is that *hussy?*"

"That hussy," I answered proudly, "is my Dad!"

A Mensch & More: The Story of Herman Liss

Michael

MY FATHER AND I WERE DRIVING TO THE SHALOM Center. "Mike, Herman's told you a lot of stories by now, hasn't he?" my dad asked.

"Yeah, he has," I agreed.

"Well, why don't you film them?"

I had some vague idea of what my father was talking about. My dad was always big on filming people's stories—something he wished he could have done when he was a kid. The idea seemed smart and rather easy. We could film Herman doing what he did every day, and then we would have something to remind us of Herman for the rest of our lives. I wasn't really sure how this would work.

"What? Will they let us—?"

"Well, I'm sure we can ask."

And that was the beginning of the movie. I went to the coffee shop and saw a now-familiar sight—Herman, sitting with his back turned, speaking to Michele.

"Dad, look who's here!" Michele began, as she typically did.

I proposed the idea immediately to Herman. "Herman, can I film you one day?" I began rather short and simply.

After some questions and conversation, Herman responded with a smile, a twinkle in his eye, and a handshake. "Sure, Mike. When would you like to begin?"

We started planning on our very next visit, and from then on our weekly meetings were transformed from leisurely chats to businesslike sessions, setting topics and preparing lists of questions.

The first day my father and I walked into the Shalom Center with high-tech equipment I felt a little weird. One of the Center's front desk receptionists looked strangely at us and then said, "Just write your names here—"

Throughout the process Herman seemed thrilled to be interviewed about his life. He was a willing storyteller. We placed him in front of a plain white wall in the Shalom Center's community room, shined a light bulb to illuminate his face, hooked a microphone to his green shirt, and let him begin.

I sat there feeling nervous.

Every morning while driving me to school my dad turned on National Public Radio, and I heard the interviewers asking intelligent, relevant questions with great ease. Like most things done by professionals, they made it sound so simple.

But I still didn't know enough about Herman to make a detailed interview. So Michele usually crept up behind me and wrote down on a sheet of paper, "Ask him about—"

Eventually we asked Michele to conduct some of the interviews. Herman's answers were thorough and informative. Herman at ninety-four was sharper than many people his age, but he still faltered. His answers were occasionally off-topic, but Michele knew him well enough to get him on track again. I was more unsure.

We showed Herman photos from his life and asked him about them. He always had a lot to say. There was one photo of him at the beach with his niece, plenty of him in Hong Kong and Morocco, Israel and Greece, Pikes Peak and Hawaii, and even some army pictures. Herman looked carefully at each photograph and told the story behind each one. I could tell that Herman felt like they were a link to his past. Herman had had such an interesting life, and looking at them, after he'd lost so much, helped him to relive it.

Herman had so much to talk about that we were never able to say, "Well, this week's the end of it—let's stop now."

After each week's interview, he always asked, "What about next week?"

"It's on for next week," we would always say.

Eventually we accumulated more than five hours of Herman on tape. The editing task felt daunting, but my father had a method for turning the tape into a cohesive film. I chopped up the footage and titled each piece according to its subject. After spending many Saturday mornings in my pajamas doing this—and becoming increasingly proficient with the video editing software—we put the most relevant pieces into the rapidly growing film.

We divided and edited the footage into five chapters: "Childhood," "The Young Man," "The Salesman" (in which Herman discussed his career and how his attention to detail and honesty led to success), "Married Life," and "The Shalom Center." Each chapter title was introduced on a black background, accompanied by Yiddish, jazz, and Israeli tunes that were Herman's favorites. In between the segments we showed interviews with his nurses, his friends, and close administrators from the Shalom Center. Herman's narration also became a voiceover for a series of photographs set to music from his collection.

The film needed a name, but a title had never crossed our minds. There seemed to be infinite possibilities—or sometimes none at all.

Sitting in the comfortable leather chair inside my father's office, I heard one of Herman's quotes: "A *mensch* is an ordinary person who would never harm anyone, who would always lend a helping hand—"

"Mensch" is a Yiddish word for something that Herman himself embodied. But the title of our film couldn't be simply *"Mensch."* Herman was more. He was a *mensch* and more. This was the story of Herman Liss.

It was perfect: *A Mensch and More: The Story of Herman Liss.*

INTEREST IN THE FILM was amazing—and growing. Each week brought more energy to the project, with all sorts of people in Herman's life volunteering for a part.

We weren't sure what to do with the material, however. We thought of making three or more different films—one completely raw version of nothing but Herman for Herman's closer relatives, another thirty-minute version for us, and then a fifteen-minute version for people totally unfamiliar with Herman. It was at this point that I felt the most confused about our project—how would we do this? My father and I sat on the couch, throwing out ideas. In the end we simply created one film, accessible to everyone.

The project eventually neared an end. It had lasted from October

2003 until mid-March 2004, approximately five months. Something that had once seemed like a far-fetched fantasy of my father's and mine was coming true—we had completed a thirty-three-minute long documentary dedicated to Herman.

The final step was to transfer the movie to VHS and DVD—that took the entire night plus a couple more hours.

So far, no one had seen the film except my immediate family. I could not wait to show the completed product to Michele and Herman. We invited Michele over one night to see the movie for the first time. At many points it looked as though she was stifling tears. I didn't think that the movie would make people cry!

We scheduled a date for the premiere—earlier than we'd expected. I thought it would be a rather informal showing to anyone who wanted to see it, but all of a sudden, with Michele's supervision, we were making programs in fancy type.

Herman still had not seen the movie. At a small get-together the weekend before the premiere, he finally did. His first reaction was very subdued. He watched it, thoughtfully furrowing his brow throughout.

I had expected a different reaction—tears, or surprise, perhaps. But Herman saw it for the first time on a small screen in a comfortable community room, with a few of his and Michele's friends who would not be able to make it to the premiere.

Once Herman was at the premiere, seeing the film on a big screen with a big audience of family, friends and caretakers, his reaction was quite different.

A MOVIE & MORE

ONE EARLY NOVEMBER AFTERNOON DAD AND I chatted in the coffee shop as we waited for Michael to arrive. A picture window framed the crimson and amber autumn explosion.

"Look at that," my father marveled. "It's like a painting. Imagine, we get to see this every year!"

"Herman, hi!" Michael exclaimed as he bounded into the room. They greeted each other with the same fusion of joy and wonder ignited every week. Michael, barely containing himself, blurted, "Herman, I have something to ask you. My father and I wonder if it would be OK with you to film the story of your life?"

"You want to film the story of my life?" Dad was incredulous.

"Yes, very much."

"Is this for a school project?" I asked, remembering that Michael had recently completed a video assignment.

"No," he said. "We think it would be great to capture Herman on film. He's seen so much change in his years and is such an amazing man. He has so much to share."

"Michael," Dad said, "if you make this movie, I would like to think it could help you in some way."

"Well, when I go away to college in a few years, I'll be able to take you with me!"

"Sure, Michael, we can make a movie!" Herman said, reflecting Michael's eagerness.

THE NEXT MONDAY the three of us had our first planning session. The movie would begin with Herman's parents' journey from Poland and then explore his childhood experiences and adolescent ambitions. Dad's work as a young journalist, his army years and bachelor days would follow. The film would capture Herman's enthusiasm for sales and his advancement to regional manager. Most important, it would highlight my parents' love story. Dad's new life at the Shalom Center, interspersed with interviews of friends, family, and staff, would conclude the film. Memories, photos, and music could create the backdrop to bring the story of Herman's life to life.

Each week Michael and his father, Ben, taped conversations with Herman, setting up their equipment in the newly refurbished family room at the end of the hall. Dad and I prepared for these sessions by looking at old pictures and reconnecting with visions and feelings of his more than nine decades. Every afternoon I'd ask questions, and we'd walk together through my father's life. It was a gift to both of us.

Dad was a natural in front of the lens. Mom used to say of him, "Herman never met a camera he didn't like!" It was the others who, when interviewed, got nervous. Herman would engage them, and soon they, too, would drop their shoulders and smile.

Lisa, Dad's social worker at the Shalom Center, sat next to my father with tears in her eyes as she was interviewed. "It's most amazing," she said. "I'm here in a role to provide support for Mr. Liss, yet I find he is my teacher instead of my being his support."

She went on to explain. "You taught me what it means to be an important member of a community and what it means to grieve the loss of someone you love. It is a blessing to realize that such a love exists."

Maria, Dad's aide from Colombia, also shared her amazement at my father. "I never met a person like Herman in my life. He's kind and funny and cares about people a lot. He sometimes forgets about himself."

She went on, "Herman loves to read. He's a very wise guy and knows a lot about life. We talk, laugh, and play. I love Herman, and my kids, nephews, and my husband all met him and love him as much as I do."

Lori, Dad's nurse, looked at him and said, "When I meet a man, hopefully he's like this guy here." The smile on both of their faces lit up the screen.

Scott, Herman's grandson since the age of three, wrote a poem about his grandfather for the film. As thirty years of candid pictures of the two of them flashed on the screen, the melody "Danny Boy" played softly in the background. Michael read the words:

My Grandpa

From the moment I first looked into your eyes,
I knew an angel had fallen from the skies.

You came into my life when I was just a boy.
Who knew you'd be more interesting than any toy?

You've always been an important presence in my life.
I thank God you chose my grandmother as your wife.

You taught me how to laugh, cheer and rejoice in what I had.
Even when I shot that arrow in the tree, you didn't get mad.

I remember fondly when we would view adult magazines
    in the mall.
I was on cloud nine—What a ball!

As I grew and started to become a man,
I would try to emulate you: You are the epitome of a human.

As I became older, I looked to you for guidance and direction
    in my life.
In part it's because of you that I decided to take a wife.

They say blood is thicker than water—that may be true,
but you're the one who holds our family together.
You truly are the glue.

I strive to be half the man you are—that is my goal.
You are always in my heart, my prayers, and my soul.

These words don't begin to describe the impact you've had on me
    over the years.
I only hope that when I have grandchildren, I will hear
    their cheers.

EXCITEMENT MOUNTED at the Shalom Center as the film was being shot and edited. One afternoon while Mike and Ben were packing their equipment, Rebecca said to me, "I think we should show this film at a Board of Directors meeting. We can all learn from it."

Hearing that, I realized that this movie could be valuable to more than our two small families. Herman had so much to teach, to share. The theme of appreciation and kindness flowing between generations and cultures and faiths is life giving.

Herman was genuine—he lived his beliefs. In his own words, he was "an ordinary man." Yet he touched others in extraordinary ways. Here was a model of how to live in the face of crisis and loss. This simple man had lost everything except for his faith and his capacity to love. He was the richest man I knew.

Perhaps, I mused, this film deserved a premiere. It would be an opportunity to share Herman's story and celebrate its message. The Shalom Center had just completed construction of a movie theater on site, so everyone who worked with Dad—who knew him, who loved him—could be invited.

The administrators enthusiastically supported this idea, and we chose a date—April 22, 2004.

THREE WEEKS before the event, the CEO of the Shalom Center approached Dad. "Herman," he said, "You're a big guy, like me. I was wondering, would you like to wear my tuxedo for the premiere? It would fit you perfectly."

My father's face lit up. "When I was younger I really enjoyed wearing a tux on special occasions. Thank you, thank you!" he exclaimed as they shook hands. The years melted away.

Sandra, the development officer, began calling newspapers and TV stations to inform them of the premiere. Each afternoon she bounded breathlessly into Herman's room to tell him who accepted an invitation. We began counting down the days on Dad's wall calendar.

Herman began to envision ways to welcome our guests. "Michele, do you think we could decorate the theater? Maybe we could make some signs thanking everyone for coming. I especially want to thank Michael and Ben for everything they've done. And I want to thank the

Shalom Center, too."

"What a great idea, Dad! Let's do signs and table decorations. We can make bright crepe paper flowers for the walls, too." The teacher in me was coming out.

Each afternoon for more than two weeks, Dad and his hospice aides cut and glued and pasted to create posters and cards of welcome and appreciation. The Shalom Center planned a festive reception to follow the showing.

There couldn't have been more joy had it been a Hollywood premiere.

THE PREMIERE

"**H**ERMAN, YOU'RE OUR KING AND NOW OUR movie star!" I heard coming from the small group of nurses and aides crowding around my Dad. Maria was wheeling him from his bath in the hall back into his room to dress for the premiere of the film *A Mensch and More.* "You know, Herman, if you were fifty years younger we'd all be fighting over you!"

"What do you mean, fifty years younger?" retorted another nurse. "We're fighting now!" Maria and Dad were both glowing as she pushed him through his doorway and caught me admiring the tux hanging on the back of the bathroom door. They greeted me with the same excitement I felt bubbling up inside.

"OK, handsome," Maria said. "First a shave and then we'll put on that gorgeous tux."

"Right," Dad laughed. "And please, let's not forget the cologne."

I waited in the room as Maria shaved my father, and heard giggles as she applied the stick deodorant she had bought him as a gift. Then came the cologne. "Herman, you smell as good as you look! OK, Michele—we're coming out, so please wait for us in the hall while Herman gets dressed."

When I left, another aide came into the room so she and Maria could help my father stand as they pulled on his pants.

"Herman, when everyone sees you dressed like this, they're going to go crazy. You'll be the best looking guy they've ever seen."

Memories of the first time I met Herman, more than thirty years before, played in my mind. "People say he looks like the movie star

Melvyn Douglas," I again heard my mom say. Even now, at nearly ninety-five, Herman was strikingly handsome. But it was more than his brilliant blue eyes and strong features. It was the broad smile, the welcoming look that said "Come sit by me awhile. I'll listen. I'll care. You matter."

The door opened. "You can come in now," Maria beamed. I helped her put on Dad's starched white shirt and studs, the cummerbund and jacket, and finally the spit-polished black leather Italian shoes.

I wheeled Dad to the mirror so he could see himself. He looked like an angel in a tux.

"Herman," Maria said, "I heard the newspapers will be here, and maybe some TV stations. We should get your autograph now while you're still talking to us."

"Maria, I can't thank you enough for all you do for me. Everyone here is so kind and does so much to help me." Dad kissed her hand before she left the room.

We were alone for a moment before we left for the premiere.

"I want you to know," Dad said, "this is happening because of Michael and Ben and you. You make my life so sweet. I'm a very lucky man."

I thought my heart would burst.

THE PREMIERE was scheduled for 3:30. Earlier in the afternoon Dad's hospice aides came in to pick up the decorations to hang in the Gazebo Theater. Along with the bags of colorful flowers and the glittered thank you signs made by Herman, I had sent a shiny red and blue wall hanging that read *"Mazel Tov!"* Hebrew for "Congratulations!"

We started down the hall at three o'clock, and everyone stopped to shake Dad's hand, kiss him, admire him. Simultaneously regal and humble, Herman was cheered by his loving court.

He and I rode the elevator down to the first floor. "Dad," I asked, "Do you have any idea how excited people are for you today?"

Herman looked reflective—almost sad. "I just wish Mom could be with us."

"She is," I replied. "*She is.*"

I pushed Dad out of the elevator and down a long, glass enclosed hallway. Light streamed in. At the end of the hall stood Michael, looking older in his navy jacket, white shirt and tie. He appeared distracted, though—somewhat uneasy in the swirl of activity around him. Then he saw Herman. His eyes sparked and that familiar smile grew wide. Mike raced toward Dad, and they shook hands, neither wanting to let go.

"Michael, you look so handsome."

"Thank you, Herman. So do you! You look great."

In that moment they saw only each other. Light bulbs flashed, but they didn't seem to notice. It was just the two of them.

Friends, staff, administrators, hospice workers, board members, journalists, and photographers stood in line to greet Herman. Exhilaration was everywhere.

"Ah," said Rachel, Dad's Queen Esther, when she took his hand. "My handsome King."

Always elegant, today Rachel was dressed in a deep grape-colored suit with earrings and brooch to match.

"And you," he responded, "make a lovely Queen." He kissed her hand.

Rachel's eyes shone and she blushed.

The guests admired the movie poster just outside the entrance to the theater. Michael had drawn a remarkably life-like picture of my father surrounded by his beloved books. The book he held was entitled *A Mensch and More*. The programs, featuring a cover designed by Herman's most ardent fan, were handed out at the door.

When all of the guests were seated, I wheeled Dad to the front row to sit next to Michael and his family. My heart was pounding with pride for this man who just eighteen months before had had his world turned upside down. In a year and a half Herman had traversed darkness and pain and became a beacon of light.

Rebecca, Director of Activities at the Shalom Center, came to the microphone and with tears in her voice spoke about the man she had come to adore. I then welcomed the enthusiastic crowd—people of diverse ages and origins and life experiences. Herman was the magnet who had drawn us together in celebration, in gratitude.

Then Michael's eleven-year old sister, Allie, read her reflections on Herman.

"Herman, I've known you only for a short time, but you have inspired me. From you I've learned what goodness can do and how beautiful generosity is. If everyone on this Earth were as kind as Herman Liss, this would be heaven. Thank you, Herman, for teaching me so much."

I wheeled Dad up to the front of the room.

"Thank you all for coming to honor me. I am very grateful for your love and caring, and appreciate what all of you have done to help me since my move to the Shalom Center. I especially want to thank Michael and Ben for making this film, for bringing it to life. And I'm going to make a prediction that Michael has a brilliant future ahead of him. Michael is a young *mensch,* and that is very rare."

Then he said, "Today I am speaking to you from this wheelchair, but I want you to know it's only temporary."

Everyone laughed and clapped.

THE FILM BEGAN and the audience responded with smiles and tears. The journalist next to me sat with notebook in hand, whispering questions, and the young female photographer who sat across from us in a corner of the room cried throughout the film. When the movie ended, there was silence, then cheers.

Michael stood to speak. He looked at Herman, and his eyes glistened.

"Herman, we named this movie *A Mensch and More* because you always say that being a *mensch* is what means the most to you. *Mensch* is the Yiddish word for a kind, true-hearted man who thinks optimistically and lends a helping hand. You've always told me that a *mensch* is an ordinary person and that it can be anyone. Herman is an ordinary man, yet he has captivated us with his wisdom, his kindness, his optimism, his love. Herman, whenever I come to see you I am surrounded by other people who have come to learn from you, who have come to laugh with you, who have come to love you. Everybody in the audience has truly benefited from knowing you. You bring out the best in everyone."

After Michael spoke, Rabbi Rosansky invited Herman and Ben to come up and join Michael for a special blessing. Father and son stood on either side of my dad's wheelchair as she asked for God's protection for all of them. Then out came the rhythm instruments, and the rabbi handed my dad a pair of maracas. The room was led in joyful song, a prayer of thankfulness. Dad swayed, shook his maracas in perfect rhythm, and sang with absolute abandon. He was dancing in his chair.

We had a reception for the guests. While they were enjoying the desserts, journalists interviewed Michael and Dad. Several made appointments for longer sessions.

This humble man, this ordinary man, truly was a star—not because he was on film, not because of media interest, but because he cared.

LIFE IS A JOURNEY

EACH TUESDAY AT FOUR O'CLOCK I JOINED A SHAlom Center staff yoga class held in the same rotunda as the film's premiere. That was also the time of Michael's weekly visit with my dad. On May 4th, nearly two weeks after the film's showing, I rushed through the building's sliding glass entrance doors, a few minutes late, yoga mat under my arm. There was Michael standing near the reception desk, looking forlorn.

"Mike—hi—have you already visited Herman?" I asked, puzzled.

"Well, I went to his room, but he's fast asleep. I don't want to wake him up, so I called my Mom to come get me, but she didn't answer the phone."

"Mike, I'll skip yoga today. Let's go back up and I'll wake Herman. He would never want to miss your visit."

As we entered the elevator and walked down the hall, people stopped us. Nurses, aides, administrators, and my dad's friends congratulated Mike on the film. They shared their joy in celebrating Herman's life and reflected on the latest newspaper articles about the premiere.

When we reached Dad's room, Jessie, his aide, was at his bedside encouraging him to drink some ginger ale. "Herman, you haven't eaten all day. Just take a few sips. You don't want to get dehydrated. Please."

He took a few swallows, certainly not because he wanted it, but because he wanted to make Jessie feel better. "Thank you very much," he said.

They saw us standing at the door. Jessie reported, "Your dad's been in bed all day. He's coughing a little, and we just gave him a breathing treatment. He had a little breakfast, but hasn't eaten since then."

"Michael, how are you?" Dad asked as he extended his hand to him. "I'm so happy to see you, and especially glad that you and Michele have a chance to visit together. "

"I'm fine, Herman. I'm so glad you're up. I thought I wasn't going to see you today. You were sleeping when I was here before."

"Oh, Mike, if you ever come and I'm napping, just wake me up. Seeing you is much more important than sleep."

Today's visit was the first since the premiere that no journalists or photographers joined them. Just that morning another feature article had appeared in a local paper.

"Herman, I see someone already brought you today's article," Michael said as he and Dad looked up at the bulletin board across from the bed. It was covered with pictures and stories about their friendship printed in the *Boston Globe,* the *Boston Herald,* the *Jewish Journal, Jewish Advocate,* and several other papers. Herman and Mike looked at each other and smiled the same expansive smile. It was as if they were twin souls born eighty years apart.

Dad beamed. "I just want to know that this film is going to help you, Michael."

"Oh, Herman, it already has, because I learned so much more about you. I learned things that I might never have known."

Marjorie, Michael's mother, poked her head in the room. "Come in and join us," I urged.

"Yes, please," said Herman. "It's so nice to see you."

"Mike, I just heard your call asking me to pick you up early. Herman, how are you?"

"I'm just a little tired, but fine."

"I'm really glad to hear that. Mike, I think I'll run a few errands and go pick up your sister while you're visiting, and then I'll come back to pick you up around five o'clock."

Marjorie turned to leave and then said, "Oh, on second thought, I think I'll stay after all. I'd really like to visit."

"I'm so glad," responded Herman.

Marjorie took a seat next to her son on the other bed.

"Herman, I want you to know that since the premiere the phone hasn't stopped ringing. All of our friends and neighbors who've read the articles have called to congratulate us," Marjorie enthused.

"That's wonderful," Dad said. "You can be very proud of Michael. I've been thinking that Michael would make an outstanding filmmaker. He's got so many talents. He writes, he's a cartoonist, and he's imaginative. No doubt Michael will be very successful one day."

"Herman, you'll be interested to hear this. Mike is getting calls about your film from people we don't even know. One woman said she read about the premiere and would like to see the movie. We also got a call from a professor who asked if he might show it to his class. Channel 7 in Boston just invited you and Mike to come in two weeks for a taping for an early Sunday morning program. Herman, this is amazing. You're a star!"

We talked and laughed and reminisced for about an hour. Dad's breathing and color returned to nearly normal. When Mike and Marjorie left for home, I stayed with Dad and encouraged him to drink some more.

"I'm sorry you didn't get to your yoga class today," Dad said. "But since you're here, would you mind filling up the feeder again? Even though I didn't eat, the birds were very hungry today."

"I had much more fun with you than going to yoga. You know, it's not every daughter who has a father who's a star," I said as I rubbed the top of his head. "But Dad, it's not just the movie—you are a star because of who you are. You light up hearts. I'm so proud of you. Do you know how good you make people feel about themselves, about life? Do you have any idea how people adore you?"

"I'm very, very lucky," Dad responded.

"It's not luck, Dad. Luck has nothing to do with it. It's you!

"You've always been my mentor," I said, "but in the past eighteen months you've been my finest teacher. See, I carry your words with me." I pulled out the small notebook I had in my purse and read his words back to him.

"You told me, 'Life is a journey, and no matter our years, it's very short and very precious. We have to make the most of every moment, because each one is a gift.'

"Most important, you said, 'happiness is appreciating all of the good in your own life—and helping to make life good for others.'

"Dad, you've made me happy every day since I've known you."

I kissed him, filled the birdfeeder, and got ready to leave for my Kabbalah lesson. "I'm going home now to have dinner before my class. Will you try to eat something tonight? Jessie will bring it in for you."

"I'm really not hungry," he responded, and closed his eyes.

"How about some chocolate ice cream—even if it's just a taste?"

"All right, thank you. That might be good."

"That's great, Dad, I'll tell her on the way out. I love you, and I'll see you tomorrow. Feel well."

"I love you, too," he said, kissing my hand.

THAT EVENING in class the rabbi explored the mystical soul. Following that we meditated on a soul journey to another dimension.

"Close your eyes and see yourself walk under the Hebrew letter *Chet*, a letter that looks like a doorway. As you make the passage, feel your spirit rise to a place of harmony and beauty." The rabbi sang an enchanting Hebrew melody to help release us.

I felt my spirit rise. It floated upward, upward toward a radiant light. A hand was extended, and I reached toward it. I was pulled close in love and joy. I was in my mother's embrace. Then my grandparents and Herman's parents appeared.

Mom said, "Honey, it's time for Dad to come home to us. It's going to be soon, and he won't suffer. We're going to come to him and bring him back with us. He'll be happy here, free. Our home is filled with light and love and peace. It's time for us to be together again."

Warm tears ran down my face. It was so real, so beautiful that I didn't want to leave.

Mom continued, "Someday we'll come back to bring you home, but now is not your time."

I floated in a celestial circle with these tender spirits, hands and hearts and souls entwined.

"When I count backwards from five, it's time for you to return," I heard the rabbi say. "Five, four, three, two, one."

But I didn't want to come back—didn't want to leave the light, the love, the mystery.

Again I heard the rabbi count "Five, four, three, two, one" and this time I felt myself re-enter my body reluctantly, yanked back too soon. I struggled to open my eyes.

"Michele, are you all right?" the rabbi asked gently. "You traveled, didn't you?"

"Yes," I whispered.

A Teacher & a Healer

THE NEXT MORNING, FOLLOWING THAT UNSETTLING and yet blessedly peaceful meditation, I cleared my schedule so I could spend the full day with my father. I wanted to be close to him, and by nine I was at the nurses' station across from his room. "How's my dad doing this morning?" I asked.

"Michele, last night Herman started wheezing a bit, and we gave him a treatment. He's sleeping comfortably now."

When I entered his room Dad's eyes were closed and his large, loving hands lay softly curled by his sides. I pulled a chair close to him and watched his chest rise and fall in unsteady rhythm. I prayed silently.

Barbara, Herman's hospice nurse, came to the door and beckoned me to the hallway. "I just read your dad's chart and spoke to the floor nurse. There was a change overnight. We'll receive the test results soon," she gently explained.

"Barbara, there's something I need to share with you." I told her about the vision I had the previous night, and we both cried. She was there for my dad, but for me as well.

Barbara hugged me with such amazing strength and love that I felt my mom's presence once again. "I'm so grateful that you're here," I cried.

"You know," she said, "I really wasn't planning to be here this morning. I was on my way to another nursing home, but the phone rang in the car. It was my husband, Geoffrey. He asked, 'Are you on your way to see Herman?' I told him no, that I saw him yesterday morning and that he looked well. Geoff responded, 'I was just thinking of Herman and wanted you to say hello for me.'"

Geoffrey had met Herman when Barbara brought him to visit one Sunday, Barbara's day off. She knew they shared a lot. Geoff was a salesman, just as Herman had been. Both were smart, sensitive men who knew how to laugh, and they felt an immediate kinship.

"When you do see Herman, tell him I was asking about him," Geoff said before he hung up.

Barbara continued, "Moments later, as I was driving to the other facility, I saw a woman walking down the street. Michele, she looked like pictures I had seen of your mother. Between Geoff's call and seeing this woman, I drove right to the Shalom Center. Actually, it felt like the car took me. No sooner did I park in the lot than the phone rang. It was your dad's nurse telling me he was in distress. She asked me to come immediately. 'I'm here!' I told her." Barbara reached out to me in a warm embrace.

We entered the room together, and she spoke softly to my dad. "Hi, Herman. How are you feeling this morning?"

He blinked his eyes, not quite opening them fully. "I'm a little tired," he whispered.

"You just rest today, and we'll give you treatments to break up the congestion. Later we'll do some tests to see what's wrong. I'll be back to check on you in a bit. And Michele, if you need me, I'll be in the next wing. Call if you need anything at all."

"Thank you," I nodded.

I sat next to my dad on his bed and kissed the top of his head.

"I was just dreaming about Mom," he told me. "Only it didn't feel like a dream. She was here in the room with my mother. They both looked beautiful and young and happy."

"What was that like, Dad—having them here?"

"Comforting," he replied, gazing over my shoulder. "The only thing is, I wish I could join them. I've had a long and happy life—a very good life. I've been so blessed. Now I dream of being with Mom. I keep seeing her in a beautiful gown, and she just floats into my arms, and we're dancing together again. I think it's only a dream, but I'm not sure. It seems so real."

He started to cough. "I don't know what's wrong with me. I'm feeling strange—different than I've ever felt before. You know I've always been healthy. I don't want to complain, but I just don't feel right. The nurses want me to eat, to drink, but I have no appetite. I'm so tired. All I want to do is sleep."

Dad closed his eyes and drifted off. When he awoke a while later, he softly said, "I want you to know how much you mean to me—how much I appreciate all you have done to make my life better. I never thought I'd have a child, and you've treated me as though I raised you. Always know how good you've been to me. I would have been so alone without you. You've watched over me as though I was your baby. I could never have managed this myself."

"Dad, it doesn't matter that I wasn't born your child. You shared more love and laughter and wisdom than most people ever know with their fathers. You're the dad I prayed for when I was little, and my prayers were answered."

"I never knew what it meant to be a father."

"Yes, you did. It's part of who you are. You were meant to be a father. It just came a little later. I remember the first time I met you, the way you looked at Mom with such amazement and delight. I remember your smile, your gentleness. I thought, 'this man could love my mom with all of his being.' And somehow I knew you could love me, too.

"From the time you and mom married, we were family. We called you Dad and Grandpa since the day of your wedding. It was simple—we loved each other. I remember the laughter, the adventures, the joy—all that we shared."

"Thank God," whispered Dad, a tear running down his cheek.

"Most of all I remember your devotion to Mom when she was ill, when she was frustrated. Because of her pain and the medication she'd say things she couldn't have meant. You never wavered in your goodness or gentleness. You'd say, 'Sweetheart, what can I do for you—what can I get for you?' You'd shop for treats that would tempt her, and you'd get up in the middle of the night to rub her legs when she called out in pain. I remember how you sat by her bedside at the hospital, day after day, week after week, even when you yourself were in pain and exhausted. You never let on."

"Your Mom was my sweetheart. Nothing was too hard. I loved her from the start. I just wish we could have had more than twenty-eight years together."

SUNSET
MICHAEL

ONE OF MY MOM'S FAVORITE CHILDHOOD BOOKS was *Harriet the Spy*, a novel written in the 1960s about a young New York City girl who keeps a notebook documenting all the people she sees and meets. In 1996 it was turned into a movie—my favorite childhood movie.

Ole Golly is Harriet's nanny, one she's had since birth. One day Ole Golly finally decides to leave Harriet, believing Harriet can make it in the world without her. In my opinion, that scene is so poignant and moving that I think of it whenever something else poignant and moving occurs. My lips widen and quiver. My face becomes tense and I can feel tears welling up. Ole Golly enters the cab and rolls up the window. Harriet, just eleven years old, runs after the cab, holding onto the small bit of window that's open. Ole Golly sheds a tear. I shed fifty. I am not afraid to admit this. Something about it really works. And it will most likely continue to work for the rest of my life.

The alarming thing about it, though, is that it was the only emotional experience that ever made me cry. Some people—many people, in fact—believe that to cry is to sacrifice your pride to a small degree. The male gender in particular is not supposed to show much emotion. Sometimes I brag about this, but most of the time I know something about it isn't right.

It is coincidental that the year the movie *Harriet the Spy* came out, 1996, was the same year my grandmother died. 1996 gave me two things to cry about. Is it right that I cried when a fictional character's beloved nanny left, but not when my Grandma died?

I remember hearing the news. I loved my Grandma—or Bubbe—with every bone in my body. I had known for a while that something bad was happening. She had cancer, and when I saw her head after chemotherapy, I told her she looked like an Indian—a little thin Mohawk of hair. I wasn't expecting death, though. It was a thought that vaguely came up once, but I comforted myself saying I'd cry so hard it would all be okay.

When I heard, I was walking down the stairs in a friend's house. I didn't cry. It wasn't as though I was so overwhelmed that I couldn't cry—the tears just weren't coming.

I walked around the house that day waiting to cry.

"How are you, Michael?" my parents asked.

I remarked casually, "Oh, I'm just sad that Bubbe died." At six years old, when many kids cry about little things, I was forcing myself to sound as though I might soon cry when my grandma died. When grownups asked me how I felt, I felt terrible for not crying. I had this sort of guilt at six years old, when many kids cry when they just stub their toe.

Through the funeral I did not shed a single tear. I wasn't sure what I should do. Should I fake crying? Perhaps that was the only option, but deep down, I knew I shouldn't be having this dilemma.

Then one day in May 2004 I was in school watching another movie. This one was intended to make people cry, as opposed to *Harriet the Spy*, which was a light-hearted kid's movie. I was squinting to read the subtitles of a movie having to do with Europe in the '30s.

I was watching the movie for an extracurricular course on foreign films for school. I still wasn't feeling overwhelmed by emotions, though. By 2004, at thirteen, I had already known for eight years that the only part of a film that could really bring out raw emotions in me was Ole Golly leaving Harriet in *Harriet the Spy*.

I felt a tap on my shoulder. There was my dad standing a few steps away from me. What a teenager's nightmare. "Get your stuff," he whispered. I felt a sudden pang of fear.

"Herman's not well," he said as we walked down the steps of my school.

Suddenly I knew. It had been a thought at the back of my mind before, though. Herman was seriously ill.

I had come in for a regular visit the day before, to review the premiere with Herman. Herman, not surprisingly, was modest about what had happened, that he had turned into something of a community hero—a positive icon everyone looked up to. As I walked into his room, however, Herman was fast asleep. Figuring I shouldn't wake him, I tried but failed to find Michele in her Tuesday yoga class at the Shalom Center, and then called my mom. A little bit later Michele saw me, and we went up to find that Herman was awake. My mother came in after a while. She wasn't sure whether or not to stay and chat or do some errands, but she decided to stay. We spoke and congratulated Herman and laughed and chatted as though nothing were wrong. Today, two days later, Herman was in a coma.

I was confused as to why my parents gave me a choice to come.

"You can stay home if you want," my mother told me. "You're not obligated to come if you don't want to."

I didn't understand what she was talking about. "I'm going, don't worry," I said quietly.

"Good for you for coming," my mom said. "You don't have to."

Of course I had to! How could I not go? Why didn't anything make sense right now?

As we were leaving, our babysitter called out to my mom, "Marjorie, I'm gonna take off now! Oh, we're a little bit low on Lysol, by the way."

"Thank you."

Nancy noticed me and said in a sympathetic tone, "Oh, sorry about your friend."

Even though that was really nice of her, I was surprised that everyone on my street— everyone in the world—wasn't running out of their doors, yelling, "What happened to Herman? Is Herman all right?"

I cried. And then Ole Golly left Harriet. But I was neither happy nor relieved that I had finally cried. This was not a Nickelodeon movie.

I HAD NO IDEA what was going to happen. I had never seen someone in a coma. That was the first thing I asked. What does a coma look like? My picture of a coma came from a movie I was shown in third grade, a famous movie about Mozart called *Amadeus*. As a little eight- or nine-year-old, I was terrified as I saw Mozart at the end lying down, cross-eyed and motionless. Would I have to see Herman like that? I wouldn't be able to stomach that.

I came into the Shalom Center, signing in the guestbook like I had so many times. Under name, I wrote "Wittner family."

"Person you are visiting," it said under the next column. I had written "H. Liss" with such pride and anticipation so many times before. I loved checking my watch, seeing the different times I arrived and left. I came in at 3:57 one day, 3:54 the next. Departures varied as well. This was part of the routine I loved.

But now, could I really say I was visiting Herman? I was superstitious not to. Quickly, before I could think otherwise, I wrote, "H. Liss" under "Person You Are Visiting" and walked away as quickly as I could.

Walking through the lobby, I greeted a few familiar faces. I waited for the elevator. I even remembered which elevator out of the two was faster and by how much time. This would have been so normal. I knew it would be different, though.

As I rode in the elevator, I nervously read the signs on the tiny bulletin board there. *Wednesday is pasta night! Kosher stuffed shells, kosher macaroni, kosher ziti, and much, much more! Plus a whole lot of fun!* For the first time I didn't laugh.

I tried to get the walk down Herman's hallway over with as fast as I could. I wiped the tears out of my eyes just before I approached the dimly lit room.

The first thing I saw in the room was not Herman. There must have been about five or six other people there. I gave Michele a quick hug. Her face was dry and solemn. She muttered something in my ear that I cannot remember. I had still not turned around to look at Herman. I purposely avoided looking toward his bed. Everybody kept thanking me.

"Oh, Michael, thank you for the movie. Oh, Michael, you were so wonderful to this man—you changed his life."

The words didn't mean anything to me anymore. They didn't seem genuine as they had before. I turned my head over at a slight angle, and there was Herman. His eyes were shut, and he was breathing loudly, as if he were having a nightmare.

I'll tell you what's happening, I told myself. *He just has a small cold and right now he's sleeping it off.*

I knew this wasn't true.

The activities director, Rebecca Shane, told me that she saw these things turn around, so perhaps Herman would wake up, and once more I would get to see him. "Just go whisper something in his ear," everyone said. I couldn't. There was nothing preventing me, and I wanted to go. It was just that I physically couldn't go over there and bring myself to say anything.

Everyone in the room, at one point or another, urged me to say something. So I walked over to Herman. Memories passed before me.

Herman, in the very same dimly lit room, telling me, "There is only one God."

"Always dance," he encouraged me to tell my sister.

"You're so lucky to go to Florida. I love Florida. It's a nice style of life."

"Michael, you're a wonderful person. You keep me current."

Herman in the coffee shop on a rainy Friday morning—both of us trying desperately to figure out a game of cards.

"Would you like to hear about what I'm reading?" he asks.

"Look over there! A cardinal at my birdfeeder! It's so good when I see one of those!"

"Is there anything I can do to help?"

"I was a playboy at heart. My nights were taken up with frivolous things."

"Yes, my grandson and I would go into the mall, and together we would read magazines with, you know, scantily-clad women."

Herman in the tuxedo. "I was always sartorially perfect," he claimed. He was. He once looked amazed that I had gotten him the wrong sweater because it didn't match his collared shirt.

The one summer I got to take Herman outside every time. He was always so considerate of me. "Is the sun shining in your eyes too much?" "Look—the trees have bloomed this year." And finally, "Goodbye, Michael. See you soon."

Why was this happening? If Herman could live to ninety-four, surely he could live to 120. That's what I remember thinking. I had once wondered if I would know Herman when I left for college. I did the math myself. Yes, of course I would. Would he ever see me excel in something? Would I be able to tell him he did help? I believed then that I would.

I didn't know whether Herman could hear me or not. People were standing all around me expecting something. All the thoughts sped through my mind like a quick slideshow. I was about to say something, but the slideshow spoke instead. In those tiny white letters at the top, I saw "*End of show. Click to exit.*"

"Herman, *mmmm mamm mmamm blbl mm,*" was essentially what came out. Nothing. Something quickly came to my mind. "And I hope I see you next week."

TOWARD THE LIGHT

IN THE EARLY MORNING FOLLOWING HERMAN'S BLOOD tests, my phone rang. It was Beth, the head nurse. She had never called me before. "Michele, I think you better come now. Herman has pneumonia. He's very ill."

Minutes later I was at his bedside. Dad was on his back, eyes and mouth closed, an oxygen tube in his nose. His breathing was labored and color chalky.

"He won't let us swab his mouth," I was told. "He's clenching his teeth."

I stroked Dad's face, kissed his forehead and cheeks, and told him I was there. His eyelids fluttered a bit, but his eyes remained closed.

"I think you should call Lori," Beth suggested. "She'd want to be here."

Herman's loving nurse had moved to a new job in another town a few weeks earlier. Before Lori left she made me promise that I'd call her if ever there were a crisis. We were losing him.

"Lori, it's Michele. Herman's not responding," I choked. I couldn't finish.

"I'm coming now," was all she said, and hung up.

Alone in the room with my father, leaning over the bed rail, I rubbed my hand over the soft, short hair on the sides of his head, just as I did every day that I was with him.

Through the haze of my tears I saw the pictures on Dad's wall, pictures that seemed so incongruous at a deathbed—Herman in his hooker outfit; Herman as a bathing beauty; Herman dressed as an angel.

There was Mike's poster of the movie premiere on the nightstand, and strung over his bed, the multi-colored sign spelling *Mazel Tov.*

My eyes drifted to Dad's monthly calendar, hung just below his bulletin board. May 6th, this very day, was circled. Dad had neatly written "Mama and Papa's *Yahrzeit,*" to remind himself that this was the anniversary of the death of both of his parents, many years apart.

The room began to fill with people. My husband, David, arrived. Stan and Barbara, Dad's beloved hospice chaplain and nurse, quietly entered, hugged me tight, and tenderly took Dad's hands. Lisa, Dad's social worker, joined us as we surrounded his bed. And then Lori entered our loving circle.

Stan placed his hand on Dad's forehead and offered a prayer of gratitude for my father's life. I knew it didn't matter to my father that this man of God had been a Catholic priest. "There is just one God," Dad's voice reminded me.

There is a Jewish bedside blessing recited before one passes, and I called Rabbi Rosansky to ask her if she would come to say the prayer for Herman.

"I'll be right there," she offered.

By the time the rabbi arrived there were a dozen people in the room. Rabbi Rosansky approached his bedside and gently placed her hand on his. There were tears in her eyes. "Herman," she said, "I'm going to say a healing blessing for you."

What she didn't say was that this ancient Hebrew prayer implores that if healing is not possible, then the soul be forgiven all of its trespasses.

I stood on the other side of Dad's bed and held his left hand. As the prayer continued, again my eyes were drawn to the date on my father's calendar and the circle around his parents' names. Then I remembered. Each year on this anniversary day, according to Jewish custom, Herman went to the synagogue to pray for their souls. The prayer, the *Kaddish,* is the same prayer that Herman recited for a full year, twice a day, after each of his parents died. He continued to perform this sacred duty of remembrance every year, even as he grew old himself. Then when it became too difficult for him to drive, I'd bring him to the synagogue or arrange to have the necessary gathering of ten Jewish people come to his home so Herman could continue to honor the memories of his beloved parents according to custom.

"Rabbi," I asked, "Can we say *Kaddish* now, right here, for my father's parents on his behalf?"

"Of course we can. We have enough people."

Rebecca brought in the *Yahrzeit* candle, a candle lit in memory of the deceased, and placed it on a table at the foot of Dad's bed.

There were twenty of us now, people of many faiths, from all parts of the globe.

I whispered in his ear, "Dad, we're going to say *Kaddish* for your parents, just as you always did. We're going to say it together in their memory."

I didn't know if Herman could hear or understand. I only knew that he would have done this for his parents if he could.

The rabbi began the ancient chant, "*Yisgadal, V'Yiskadash, Shmae Rahbah—*"

A light filled the room, a light that streamed through the windows, played on the ceiling, and glistened on soft tears.

After the *Kaddish*, Lori put down the side rail to Dad's bed and slid her small body right next to him. "Herman, it's Lori."

His eyes fluttered open three times and then closed. She placed her tiny hand into his large one. He responded with a slight grasp.

Lori held him and lovingly caressed his chest, his face, his arms. "Herman," she whispered, "I want you to know, I met a man just like you." At that moment, there was another faint squeeze.

As people began to leave the room, Rebecca took me aside. "I'm wondering," she asked. "Do you think we should call Michael?"

My heart lurched. Should Michael be here? Would Dad want him to see him like this? Would Dad want this to be Michael's last memory of him? Would his parents want their thirteen-year-old son to experience this sorrow? What would Michael want?

"Rebecca, please call Marjorie at work and ask her and Ben to decide." I knew I couldn't make that phone call.

MICHAEL AND HIS PARENTS arrived at the Shalom Center in the early afternoon. By now Herman's coma had deepened, and there was no response when Marjorie took his hand. Tears streamed down Michael's face as he paced back and forth shaking his head. We stood silent guard around Dad's bed, Marjorie, Ben and I.

Michael approached Herman tenderly and placed his hand on his. With lips quivering, he whispered in Herman's ear.

Ben hugged me as they left and softly said, "He waited until the film was done, until we could have our celebration. He did it for us."

Lisa, Dad's social worker, entered the room pushing a Care Cart. There were cold drinks and hot coffee, small sandwiches, lotion, and a CD player and discs on the stand. "You might want to play some music for Herman. It can be very soothing."

"Do you really think that would be OK?" I asked.

"Of course. I think he would like that," Lisa gently responded.

I looked through the CDs. Most were classical, orchestral, or New Age ethereal melodies. Then I saw one that made me smile. It was Benny Goodman's big band music. These were the songs Dad loved— music that made his fingers snap and body sway, even in his wheelchair.

I wondered, is it a sacrilege for me to play big band music now— music with such pulse, such life, just as Dad's own life was ebbing?

Play it, I thought I heard, *and play it loud!*

I went over to my father and held him. "Dad," I said, "yesterday you told me that your fondest wish is to open your arms and dance with Mom again. She's waiting for you, Dad. I'm going to play your favorite music, and you can dance together now."

The lively sounds of trumpet and sax, violin, piano and drums drifted from the room and down the hall. Then, at the end of the recording, an enchanting voice sang the haunting song *Somewhere Over the Rainbow.*

We lost our king as the sun rose the next morning. Herman passed peacefully, just as he had lived.

THE
BIKUR CHALEM SHUL
MICHAEL

A S WE DROVE TO HERMAN'S FUNERAL, RAINDROPS began to patter quickly against the windshield. My family was traveling along some dismal-looking interstate, looking at the blooming trees, and listening only slightly to some book on audiocassette.

"What's New Haven like?" I asked.

"It's a college town. Kind of blah, sometimes," one of my parents said.

"Okay," I responded.

I was feeling strangely normal. Nothing was bothering me too much, except the Buick from Florida in front of us going at a snail's pace on the highway.

"Ben, switch lanes," my mom insisted. "The car ahead of us is, like, three trillion years old."

My dad quickly switched lanes as the rain began to fall in earnest. It sounded loud enough to smash our windowpane. It was one of those odd storms in that for five minutes it's the heaviest rain you've ever seen, and then the sun comes out.

We drove through Connecticut, which in my experience consists only of highways dotted with Exxon stations and McDonald's. Until recently it had never occurred to me that anyone even lived in Connecticut. I thought it was just the grueling, never-ending part of our frequent Boston/New York trips.

This time was no different, except that we took the exit into New Haven. We saw an old mill covered with graffiti next to a dumpster, looking out at us as though it had lived a hard life and wanted us to share its pain.

We stopped at a Dunkin Donuts. As we walked out carrying jelly doughnuts, low fat milk, and coffee, my dad looked around the gloomy area and asked, "I wonder if the Bikur Chalem Shul is still here."

"Oh, my," reflected my mom.

Herman became a bar mitzvah at the Bikur Chalem Shul in 1922, five years before my grandmother was even born. He spoke lovingly about the shul in the movie.

In my mind, the Bikur Chalem Shul was one of those synagogues from the old country—ancient, musty, and distant. The synagogues I was familiar with sponsored walk-a-thons, annual phone-a-thons, and Jewish Federation run-a-thons. Rabbis wore Nike tracksuits and the Temple Sisterhood sponsored seminars on "Losing Weight the Jewish Way." I imagined that the Bikur Chalem Shul, even in its time, was not a part of the Jewish community I knew. Just its name, unpronounceable even to many modern Jews, seemed to signify a place of purer study and learning, where old bearded men sat reading Torah and chanting ancient, sad melodies.

I wondered how long it had been since Herman himself went to the Bikur Chalem Shul. He spoke very, very little of his early childhood— because to him, thirteen was early childhood, even though for me it had only been last year—and so I wondered how many memories he actually had.

The air was warm with the kind of moist heat that follows a rainstorm. The rather abrupt change from heavy downpour to sunny, humid weather seemed like a small, helpful sign. Almost.

I felt weird standing there, across from the cemetery, in a suit. I feel weird in general walking anywhere in public in a suit, but there I felt like a businessman waiting for a train—an invisible train that would take me to the Bikur Chalem Shul to meet the Herman I never met. It would be nice if such a train existed.

But the train never came.

SAILBOATS
MICHAEL

MICHELE WAS STANDING WITH A GROUP OF PEO-
ple in a vacant lot across the street from the cemetery. We
were in Connecticut, but it felt like a ghost town in the
Old West, it was so isolated.

It was the first time I had seen Michele since Herman had gone. I
didn't know how I was going to greet her. I wasn't at Coffee at Maddie's
anymore, seeing Herman's bald head from the back, deep in conversation with his daughter, discussing Kabbalah or teaching her how to
read Hebrew. I had never been to a funeral where I was expected to say
something correct and soothing and kind—rather, I went to my last
funeral when I was six and could say whatever I wanted.

Should I read a poem or say something, I wondered? Could I go up
there and think of something impromptu? No, it wasn't a good idea.
I couldn't gather all the right thoughts in my mind and possibly turn
them into a speech. I wish I could've said something.

The cemetery looked barren and foreign. I felt like I was in a foreign
country. Many of the people gathered in black were those I had never
seen before. I listened as eulogies were read, all of them registering
somehow with me. Crying here was not an issue—it never even crossed
my mind. I was numb.

Barbara, Herman's dear hospice nurse, read the following poem by
Henry Van Dyke as a eulogy, something so beautiful that it almost
erased my numbness.

198

A Parable of Immortality

I am standing on the shore as a great ship gently glides from the harbor and sails toward the horizon. She is beautiful. Sails billowing, and shining bright as the sunlight sparkling on the distant waters. She grows smaller and smaller until at last, her white sails shine as ribbons out where the sky and water mingle as one.

As I watch, a voice behind me cries, "Well, she's gone. She's gone."

Gone? No, I tell myself. No, she is not really gone. Not really. She is gone only in the sense that I can no longer see her.

In reality, she is the same as ever, just as beautiful, just as shining. And deep in my heart I know that on another shore someone is crying out: "Look! Look, everyone! Here she comes!"

And that is dying.

I had never shoveled dirt on a grave before. I never knew the custom existed until I watched some movie in which they did that, and my mom cried, "Ooh, I didn't know they were Jewish!"—that's always a source of excitement for my mother. When I first heard about it I was shocked. That sounded like a rather disrespectful custom. Muslims won't let anyone with shoes enter their mosques because dirt might come in—why would you shovel it on a dead loved one?

I heard that the reason behind this custom is that the sound the dirt makes as it cascades onto the grave is the sound of reality—a way to really understand that there has been a death. You are saying good-bye to this person right now.

Though it sounded odd when I first heard it, after shoveling dirt on Herman's grave, it all made sense. At first I felt stronger, older, lifting up the heavy metal shovel, something that maybe I couldn't have done a few years ago. But then it was just sad—knowing that Herman was beneath the dirt and not reading the latest copy of *Newsweek,* or a book about the Jewish Mafia in the 1920s, or watching the birds by the birdfeeder.

I shoveled the dirt onto his grave, hauling the huge metal instrument over my shoulder, and thought, *My chances are up. I will never see him again in this life.* It all became real.

Then it struck me. I have to remember that Herman may have been the oldest man I knew, but he was also one of the most spirited. In spite of great loss and sorrow and illness, Herman didn't wallow away in despair—he made an uphill climb. It brings you to that classic question—is someone born a hero, or do they become a hero?

Did I help Herman live life again in his time at the nursing home, a place where most people go to die? Or was he just like that?

It brought me back to the dimly lit room, the first time I ever saw Herman. A knock on his door, and there was Herman with a peaceful expression. "There is only one God."

And April 22, when Herman rolled down the aisles of a rehabilitation center treated as royalty, dressed like royalty, with a beaming grin on his face.

For Herman, for me, the movie, the publicity, the happiness, the anticipation, was like a surprise ending—an entirely new story about to happen.

Then I realized that this didn't need to happen only to Herman. Why couldn't many more people make surprise endings for people, so others in nursing homes could go out in a bang—so, to speak—dressed in tuxedoes, making speeches, and decorating thank-you cards?

The shovel was still in my hand. But I continued to think, because this would be the closest I would ever be to him, perhaps ever again. We had had so many chats in the coffee room—about life, death, religion, humor, anything. He was a brother, a father, a teacher, an inspiration, and a generous friend, all mixed into one.

I put the shovel down, still reflecting. I walked to the back of the line and wondered if Herman knew everything I was thinking about.

I could hear his voice, loud and clear. "Michael, is there anything I can do to help?"

"Herman, you already have."

HERMAN'S HEAVEN

HERMAN HAD SHARED HIS WISHES FOR A SIMPLE graveside funeral to be attended by our small family. What he didn't realize was how our family had grown—that others loved him as a dad, an uncle, a grandpa, a treasured friend. So many who adopted Herman as their own drove four hours in torrential rain to say goodbye.

When my father first lapsed into a coma, the day before he died, I wondered if he and God had arranged for his passing to happen on the anniversary of his parents' deaths. I believe I got my answer. Amazingly, the funeral fell on the supremely joyful Jewish holiday Lag B'Omer, a day of Divine Rapture. It is told in the Zohar, the very essence of Kabbalism and a spiritual expression of the first five books of Moses, that this was the day of the passing of the blessed Rabbi Shimon Bar Yochai, a second century Israeli mystic. Rabbi Shimon, on the day of his death, was granted the holy privilege of sharing the secret of the universe. On this sacred day he revealed that the world is comprised of sparks of light, and each spark is connected to every other spark. Each one of us shines our light upon every other soul. We are linked; we are inseparable.

In Israel, there is jubilation on Lag B'Omer. Campers light bonfires in the mountains. There is dancing in the streets. Even the funerals are joyous on this holy day. How perfect!

Just as we climbed the steps to reach Herman's grave, the clouds parted and the sun streamed through the mist. A rainbow—there was a rainbow! We prayed, read poems, shared memories, and sang Herman to heaven. Rabbi Rosansky led us in a service that was exuberant, a funeral befitting the holiday and the man.

THE NEXT AFTERNOON at the Shalom Center, scores of people came to pay their respects at the shiva, the Jewish memorial gathering. They stood in line to embrace my family and share their private Herman stories. Friends, hospice workers, administrators, volunteers, and staff laughed and cried and held each other in their loving connection to my father. They came to honor the man who honored them. Each, in their own words, exclaimed, "Isn't it miraculous that Herman, just two weeks ago, celebrated his life with all of us. How many people hear how much they are loved before they die?"

Toward the end of the afternoon Rebecca, the activities director, rushed into the room and to the head of the line. Breathless, she grabbed my hand and said, "Michele, you've got to come with me. I have something to tell you!"

I excused myself and we went into the hall.

"You're not going to believe this! I just received a call from the North Shore Association of Volunteerism. Do you remember that a few weeks before the premiere the Shalom Center nominated Michael for the Student Volunteer of the Year Award?"

"Yes," I exclaimed, catching her excitement.

"Michele, Michael won! There will be an award ceremony and presentation of a scholarship next month."

Toward evening, Michael and his mom came to join us at the shiva. As we hugged each other, we remembered Dad's words. "Michael, I just want to know that this film is going to help you."

Herman was with us. He knew!

AT HOME THE NEXT DAY, the first time I was alone since Dad's passing, I still felt numb, disbelieving. I really hadn't cried. The ceaseless activity and the surreal experience of a joyful funeral hadn't given me the time or space to connect with my loss. I sat at the breakfast table distractedly leafing through the newspaper. Then I saw it. Herman, handsome, dressed in his tuxedo, beamed up at me from page ten. Here was another article about the premiere, just published.

I was taken by surprise. I didn't expect to see his picture, to feel his delight. I laid my head on the table and sobbed. Within moments I heard tapping on the glass sliders leading out to the second story deck overlooking the harbor. I didn't lift my head. Again, tap, tap, tap. I looked up, and sitting on the railing of the deck was a robin, fat and red-breasted. It flew from the rail to the slider just feet away and tapped the glass with its beak. Again and again the robin tapped and flew back to its post.

A robin, how odd. I'd never before seen a robin on my porch. They are not ocean birds. And never, ever, had a bird tapped on my glass. I stood up and walked a straight path from the dining room table through the living room to the deck, all the while talking to this eager little creature. My movement didn't frighten it.

"Dad?" I whispered. "Did you send this little bird back to say good-bye?"

The bird stared at me, chirped, and hopped on the railing to face the water. It flew heavenward.

THREE WEEKS LATER I received an ecstatic call from Rebecca.

"Michele, Michael just won another award for his work with your father. This is unbelievable! Michael has been named the Massachusetts Aging Services Association Volunteer of the Year. This award is truly prestigious, and many, many adults throughout the state who have volunteered for years were nominated, but Michael won! The award ceremony will be held in the fall."

In the meantime, community centers on the North Shore were inviting us to present the film and discuss my father's gift of light and life and love. At each showing we heard rustling as tissues were retrieved from pockets and purses. Following the film one woman told us that her mother was celebrating her 82nd birthday that day, and they were going to have dinner together.

"I want you to know," she said, "the film has given me a fresh perspective, a different way to approach my mom and sweeten our relationship. I'm going to tell her how much I care, tell her what she means to me. I understand now—no one knows how long they have. Now is the time to tell her, before it's too late!"

ON OCTOBER 7, 2004, five months to the day of Herman's passing, Michael received the Volunteer of the Year Award from the Massachusetts Aging Services Association. The occasion was the 50th anniversary of Mass Aging, an organization that serves as the voice for non-profit providers of elder services throughout the state. Three hundred people attended this elegant event, which included a reception, a keynote address by the CEO of the national association, a gourmet feast, and the awards presentation.

Michael was asked to bring a clip of the film *A Mensch and More* to serve as an introduction to the presentation of his award. Following the clip, the presenter read from Michael's nomination submitted by the Shalom Center.

"Michael and Herman, separated by eighty years, were united by their hearts. They were mirrors of each other's souls. Their relationship began with equal trepidation. Michael believed that the elderly were shriveled and limited, and Herman despaired, 'He's only a boy. What am I going to do with him?' What they did was to create magic!"

He continued, "A *mensch*, in Jewish tradition, is a person of integrity, goodness, honesty, and kindness. Michael Wittner, like Herman Liss, is himself a *mensch*. For his heart, for his vision, for honoring the wisdom of years, Michael Wittner is a most worthy recipient of the Volunteer of the Year Award."

Three hundred people jumped to their feet and cheered. Michael gazed upward.

Herman's voice echoed through that hall.

EPILOGUE
MICHAEL

LAST NIGHT I HAD A DREAM ABOUT HERMAN. IT WAS the second one since his passing a few weeks earlier, and I just turned fourteen. In a way, I anticipated having this dream. When my grandma died nine years ago, I had dreams about making her come back in some form or another. My parents told me dreams were the brain's way of expressing grief and regret. I knew that it was bound to happen with the second major loss in my life.

Dreams are what the brain weaves when no one is watching. They tell the truth.

Whenever somebody asked me how I felt about Herman, or about Herman's passing away, I always felt constrained to say the right thing—something that would sound correct, something that would sound wise but wouldn't offend. When asked, I was always slightly afraid that what I was saying wasn't what I was truly thinking.

But the dreams verified everything. It meant that all the sweet stuff I said to everyone, no matter how clichéd it may have sounded, was not a lie.

When describing the two dreams, I'm afraid I'm going to sound like one of those spiritual self-help people on television. I usually change the channel when I hear one of them. I almost want to roll my eyes, and they're my own dreams! And yet, the dreams are still what they are.

Though many non-related things happened in these dreams, I can only remember the bits about Herman.

The first took place in a familiar setting. I needed to talk to Herman once more. It was as though I was going for another weekly visit, and then I remembered. It was just as painful as it had been in real life. I couldn't see Herman. It was physically impossible to go back and talk as I had done. I would never resume the friendly visits, the soothing, predictable routine. The want in the dream was just as real as it had been in real life. I needed to speak to Herman.

So in my dream I telephoned him using the phone in my parents' bedroom. I knew that I wouldn't be able to reach him, but I dialed a strange combination of numbers, and I made a big deal over dialing one extra number at the end. That must have done it. Herman picked up.

I had called Herman in heaven, and it was just as though I was calling him in real life. I don't remember what we talked about, but his voice sounded the same, and his friendliness remained. We just spoke, the same as we had before when I came to visit. The only problem was the phone rates to heaven. They must be very expensive.

I felt the same way when I woke up from that dream as I do right now. I felt myself tearing up. One of the worst feelings is waking up from a dream that seems so real. The reality is so close, but just slightly out of reach.

The second dream was almost the same. I was leaning over Herman's coffin. It sounds morbid, but it wasn't. Herman was just lying there, as he had been the day before he passed away. Asleep. Only this time I knew he wouldn't wake up. I felt the same need to have a friendly chat with him one more time. I put my hand to his, just as I had the day before he died.

"Herman?" I asked.

"Michael," he said.

It was a miracle. His mouth wasn't moving. His frozen state remained. And then he began to speak again, but his mouth never moved. He told me about this friend and that nurse, putting in a word of praise for everyone. I didn't know where the voice was coming from.

I jumped to the conclusion that he was alive. I thought that this had all been a mistake, and I needed to tell someone. My father stopped me, though.

"Herman is still gone," he said. "That's his soul talking to you. His soul isn't dead, but his body is."

That was why his mouth wasn't moving. Nobody knows where that voice, his soul, was.

I again woke up from that dream shaken but hopeful. I had let Herman slip quickly past my fingers once more.

In both of these dreams I had found an alternate way of communicating with Herman. I shared these dreams with Michele, who had always felt, since his death, as though Herman was communicating with us in one way or another.

I think my father summed it up well in my second dream. His body may be gone, but his soul lives on.

EPILOGUE
MICHELE

"**P**LEASE, PULL UP A CHAIR AND LET'S WATCH the birds for a while," my father beckoned on an afternoon visit one week following the film's premiere. Together we sat, hand in hand, in sweet silence.

Herman began to speak, gently, confidently, "You know, I've been thinking. I've had a wonderful life, but no one lives forever. It makes me so happy to know that after I'm gone you won't be alone. You have your family and friends, and now even more friends since I've come here to the Shalom Center."

He went on. "Michael and his family, my hospice nurse Barbara, and the Angel who floated into my room after Mom died—they will all be close to you, you'll see."

This made no sense. We were still high from the movie showing, newspapers continued to call for interviews, there were scheduled television talk show dates for Herman and Michael, and a graduate school of music issued an invitation to teach about the film's score. Why was my father dwelling on this now? He looked strong and healthy and very much at peace. Anyway, why would he think that my relationship with the Wittners and Barbara and Jane would continue? After all, I only saw Mike and his parents at the Shalom Center, and the same was true for Barbara. And as for his chaplain, Jane Korins, I hadn't seen her in the eighteen months since his discharge from the hospital. We were all acquaintances brought together by circumstance.

"By the way," questioned Herman, "are you and the Angel friends yet?"

"No, Dad. The last time I saw Jane was just before you moved here." It was the same answer I gave each time he asked.

"I'm surprised," he replied, tilting his head. "You live in the same town and she's such a wonderful person. You're so much alike. You'd really enjoy each other."

"Dad, Jane is incredibly busy. She's the Director of Pastoral Care for several hospitals, trains student chaplains, and is active on lots of committees. She has very little time, I'm sure."

Herman gazed out the window and smiled, "You and the Angel will be very important to each other one day. You'll see."

ONE WEEK LATER my father died. He was right about the Wittners and Barbara. Their warm presence supported my small family at the graveside funeral held out-of-state.

The following month Michael turned fourteen, and my husband and I invited his family to dinner in honor of his birthday and his recognition as the 2004 North Shore Student Volunteer of the Year.

In the restaurant overlooking Marblehead Harbor, Michael and I reminisced about Herman and mused about collaborating on a book about his shining spirit. We wanted to share Herman's philosophy of *Tikkun Olam,* the Jewish imperative to repair the world through kindness, respect, and charity.

Every two weeks for more than a year we met to explore Herman's compassion and our writing. Our families grew close.

Herman's prediction about Barbara Goddard, his hospice nurse, was also accurate. Calls and visits and deep caring unfolded. In time, Barbara chose to pursue spiritual study and asked permission to present a teaching about Herman to her fellow students.

Barbara and Michael remained precious gifts, but sixteen months after Herman's prophecy, there was still a missing piece. Dad's angel and I had not reconnected. It was nearly three years since Jane and I had last seen one another.

When she floated back into my life, the circumstances were beyond explanation.

IN AUGUST 2005 I had begun studying to become a spiritual director, a guide for people seeking a deeper connection to a higher power.

The two-year mentor training program at the Claritas Institute for Interspiritual Inquiry required that I, myself, work with a spiritual director. I wanted to find a mentor, preferably a woman, schooled in Jewish mysticism. The Institute gave us five weeks to select our guides and report their credentials for approval.

I was provided the names of three women who matched my needs. Each lived in California and was willing to do the work over the phone. The school asked that I submit my decision by September 15.

My style as an action-oriented student was to complete assignments long before the deadline. To my amazement, I didn't call anyone on the list. I meditated and prayed that the perfect director would appear.

It made no sense. Weeks passed and I discovered four more people qualified to be my mentors. These directors worked in the Boston area, and if I selected any one of them my sessions could be face to face rather than by phone. Still I was immobilized.

I longed for the right guide to be revealed, yet I sat in inertia. There were just two weeks left.

On Labor Day weekend, intending to be productive, I sat down at my computer to do yet another search. Soon I became distracted and decided to check the weather online. It was obviously a dry, sunny day, and really, I had no need to know any more than that. Having never checked the weather on line, I decided to just type in www.weather.com and see what would happen. Only I got as far as www.w and a site popped up.

It was www.wise.org, a website for a local Women's Inter-Spiritual Experience—WISE. The organizer was described as a chaplain trainee at Salem Hospital, the hospital where my father had been admitted after his stroke.

Although I didn't know her, I wondered if *she* might be the one I had been praying for. But I had no idea if this woman was a spiritual director, nor if she had a background in Jewish mysticism. Then it occurred to me—call Jane Korins, my father's hospital chaplain and the director of pastoral care at Salem Hospital. She'd know!

In the message I left on Jane's office answering machine, I introduced myself as Herman Liss's daughter. "I don't know if you remember me," I said, "but I would appreciate some information about your chaplain trainee regarding her skills as a spiritual director."

In a return message on my machine, Jane warmly praised her student chaplain, assuring me that she would make an exceptional mentor. Then Jane said, "Coincidentally, I am going to be *her* spiritual director for the coming year."

I knew, of course, that Jane was a gifted chaplain, but didn't know that she was also a spiritual director. My heart raced. I reasoned that if the student chaplain is so insightful and she chose Jane as her director, why not ask Jane to be mine?

This time I sent an e-mail with my request. I explained that I was in a spiritual direction training program and would be grateful if Jane would accept me as a directee. Her response was somewhat guarded. She wrote that she would be happy to meet with me the following week to discuss this, but was not certain that it would be feasible for her to be my mentor. Our meeting date was scheduled just two days before I had to report my decision to the school.

When I entered Jane's office, her loving eyes and kind smile evoked my father's description of the angel who floated into his room. I had thought he called her that because he couldn't remember her name. I realized then that I was wrong.

We talked about my dad and his soul journey. Jane and I marveled at Herman's growth and resilience, his ultimate emergence as a beacon in a community darkened by loss and despair. "You know, Michele, I have had the privilege of meeting thousands of people in times of deep soul struggle, but Herman Liss is the one I remember most vividly. There are times when I am in need, and I feel his presence. I still see his gentle blue eyes, his everlasting love for his wife, his profound compassion."

I told Jane that Herman, an Orthodox Jew, was recently described by a Christian mystic with the Buddhist term *Bodhisattva*. Jane smiled and nodded her head. "A *Bodhisattva* is a holy person who returns to this world to lift others along their soul journey. That was Herman!

"Herman's life," Jane said, "was a blessing. He pointed the way for the rest of us to find our reason to get up once again, to never lose hope, to truly experience life in all of its stages, even in the midst of adversity. His love, his courage, his humor, and his zest for life will continue to illuminate and guide others. Herman's light will never be extinguished."

"Jane, these words remind me of what it means to be fully human as described in the Kabbalah. My father and I began our studies of Jewish mysticism just months before he died."

"Although I'm not Jewish," Jane replied, "Jewish mysticism calls to me. For years I've been a serious student of Kabbalah. Your father lived its precepts."

I caught my breath. "Jane, I'm here to ask you to be my spiritual director to help me prepare to do my own work in this field."

"Michele, there's something you need to know. Although I've been a chaplain for many years, like you I am now in a formal training program studying spiritual direction. I must mentor two people to receive my certificate. I am working with the woman you inquired about and have been praying for one more person, just the right person, to appear. I've asked clergy of all faiths if they might know of someone wanting spiritual direction, but no one did. No one."

Jane continued, "When you called and explained that you are also in training, I wasn't certain that I would qualify to be your mentor according to your school's guidelines. You see, I won't receive my certificate in spiritual direction for another few months."

"Yes, but you've been guiding people in spiritual awareness for your entire career," I replied. "That's what matters. That's what the school cares about."

I explained, "Jane, I, too, have been praying for just the right spiritual director, and I must report her name to my school by September 15th. Today is the 13th."

"Michele," Jane whispered, "I also need to report the names of my two directees to my school by September 15th."

We stared at each other in awe, in absolute silence. Energy swirled around us and through us, and I heard.

"One day you and the Angel will be very important to each other— You'll see!"

THE TWELVE NEVERENDING TRUTHS OF HERMAN LISS

1. Have Faith.

2. Love Tenderly.

3. Respect Everyone.

4. Express Gratitude.

5. Embody Kindness.

6. Embrace Hope.

7. Forgive Fully.

8. Invite Joy.

9. Be Curious.

10. Treasure Life.

11. Live Now.

12. Know Yourself.

Michael's Reflections

EVEN THOUGH THE BOOK YOU'RE READING WAS PUB-
lished in 2012, the bulk of it was actually written in 2004
and 2005, when I was fourteen and fifteen. When I was a
junior in college, I reread the book—*my* book—because sometimes I
forget. The experience of rereading it was so surreal that I was moved
to write the following reflection.

My childhood was well-documented. I was lucky to have a dad who
was good with a camcorder—as a young kid I remember thinking he
was a cyclops because his left eye was always obscured by a videocam-
era. My mom went through a period where she made boxes—the 1998
Box, the 2001 Box. She'd throw everything significant into the box—
she didn't

catalogue it, but she saved it. I like it better that way—the boxes
were fecund. When I rewatch newly digitized footage, or dive into the
1999 box as if it were a pile of autumn leaves, it's remarkable how divorced I've become from that reality. I watch another person. I listen to
the intricate imagination of *some kid.*

I often remember the events going on, strangely enough, but as
a kid, your perception of the world is different. You know there's a
grownup world—you see the grownups talking in

hushed whispers about things you'll know about *when you're older*—
and now I've gotten there. I can see how I looked to them.

Rereading the book, I sometimes felt the same way. I just wished I
could write about an experience I understood better.

Even at sixteen I was upset that I couldn't make sense of what was going on because I was too young. Late one night I e-mailed Michele in a frenzy. "If I knew Herman now, we could have talked about so much more! I didn't know anything back then!"

That's my experience with this book, all these years later—I don't know who wrote it. I remember writing it, I remember my life at the time, but in six years, I've changed.

An anthropology professor once asked our class: "Think of yourselves at age eleven. Are you the same person now that you were then?" Our hands all shot up, and then, as we really considered the question, we slowly lowered them. Yes, no, maybe, sort of—

Make no mistake. This text was written by Michael Wittner. But was it?

I was under the mistaken impression that adults know more than kids do. If you have a driver's license, if you can drink legally, if you've been to college, the relationships you'll have will be more real and more meaningful. I couldn't express myself as well back then. Sometimes I didn't really understand what Herman was saying. But intuitively, I think, I understood everything. And the more I read my passages of the story, the more I realize that in my own way, I communicated everything that mattered.

AFTER YOU WATCH a movie you really like, it's hard to remember the details. I find that it's surprisingly easy to speak at great lengths about how the movie made you feel. Ultimately, this story brings me back to a time in my life that was pleasant. It helps me remember the feeling I got when I walked into Herman's room and he realized that I was there. God, that greeting.

Back then my life was optimistic and innocent. The writing gives me *the feeling*—I don't know how else to describe it. But I imagine that most people know, on an intuitive level, what I'm describing—when you're listening to a beautiful song in a beautiful place, let's say, and everything goes up to the next level. *Feelings*. I don't know whether I believe in God with a capital G, or any power at all. I don't think I can ever know or understand, and I'm okay with that. For now, those *feelings* are as close to some sort of higher power as I think I'm ever gonna get.

Back then I had the *feeling* all the time. I don't have it as much now. I have fun. I travel. I meet cool people and do cool things with them. My life is pretty good. But it's nice to be pulled back to a time in my life that was—well—I guess it was transcendent.

Isn't that what writers are supposed to do? Define the indefinable? It's asymptotic—I think by definition, artists produce representations, imitations, impressions, and those aren't real. But the good artists can get pretty damn close.

When I reread what I wrote, after I stop nitpicking and see it for what it is—a young kid writing about what happened to him—and not for what I think it should be—which is God knows what—I'm moved. I don't know who wrote it, and I don't know how he did it, but he moved me. He gave me a glimpse into his beautiful little world— and I really think it was a beautiful world—and through words, he let me know how he felt about it, and invited me to try it out.

And perhaps, I'm starting to think, did it better than I could do now.

MICHAEL WITTNER
January 2012

About the Authors

Michele Tamaren

Michele Tamaren, M.A. is a writer, presenter, spiritual mentor, and life coach. She lectures widely on spirituality, healing, and happiness, as well as compassionate care and spiritual growth at the end of life. Michele engages audiences of medical personnel, psychologists, social workers, chaplains, clergy, spiritual mentors, and professional and family caregivers.

For more than twenty-five years Michele taught special education, working with youngsters challenged by physical, learning, social, emotional, and behavioral disorders. She presented self-esteem and anti-bullying workshops throughout the United States and Canada.

Michele is the founder of the multi-faith Council for Spiritual Connection, which brings together those of all traditions to celebrate our shared humanity. In 2010 she was presented with the Anti-Defamation League's Leonard P. Zakim Humanitarian Award for fostering interfaith harmony.

Visit her at www.micheletamaren.com.

Michael Wittner

Mike Wittner just graduated from Bard College with a B.A. in sociology. Next year he will be teaching in underserved schools as a part of the City Year Americorps Program. He likes to read, write, think about politics, and take long walks, preferably all at the same time.

ABOUT PEARLSONG PRESS

PEARLSONG PRESS IS AN INDEPENDENT PUBLISHING COMPANY dedicated to providing books and resources that entertain while expanding perspectives on the self and the world. The company was founded by Peggy Elam, Ph.D., a psychologist and journalist, in 2003.

Pearls are formed when a piece of sand or grit or other abrasive, annoying, or even dangerous substance enters an oyster and triggers its protective response. The substance is coated with shimmering opalescent nacre ("mother of pearl"), the coats eventually building up to produce a beautiful gem. The self-healing response of the oyster thus transforms suffering into a thing of beauty.

The pearl-creating process reflects our company's desire to move outside a pathological or "disease" based model of life, health and well-being into a more integrative and transcendent perspective. A move out of suffering into joy. And that, we think, is something to sing about.

PEARLSONG PRESS ENDORSES Health At Every Size, an approach to health and well-being that celebrates natural diversity in body size and encourages people to stop focusing on weight (or any external measurement) in favor of listening to and respecting natural appetites for food, drink, sleep, rest, movement, and recreation. While not every book we publish specifically promotes Health At Every Size (by, for instance, featuring fat heroines or educating readers on size acceptance), none of our books or other resources will contradict this holistic and body-positive perspective.

We encourage you to enjoy other Pearlsong Press books, which you can purchase at www.pearlsong.com or your favorite bookstore. Keep up with us through our blog at www.pearlsongpress.com.

FICTION:

The Falstaff Vampire Files—paranormal adventure by Lynne Murray
Larger Than Death—a Josephine Fuller mystery by Lynne Murray
Large Target—a Josephine Fuller mystery by Lynne Murray
The Season of Lost Children—a novel by Karen Blomain
Fallen Embers & *Blowing Embers*—Books 1 & 2 of The Embers Series,
paranormal romance by Lauri J Owen

The Fat Lady Sings—a young adult novel by Charlie Lovett
Syd Arthur—a novel by Ellen Frankel
Bride of the Living Dead—romantic comedy by Lynne Murray
Measure By Measure—a romantic romp with the fabulously fat
by Rebecca Fox & William Sherman
FatLand—a visionary novel by Frannie Zellman
The Program—a suspense novel by Charlie Lovett
The Singing of Swans—a novel about the Divine Feminine
by Mary Saracino

ROMANCE NOVELS & SHORT STORIES FEATURING BIG BEAUTIFUL HEROINES:

by Pat Ballard, the Queen of Rubenesque Romances:
Dangerous Love | *The Best Man* | *Abigail's Revenge*
Dangerous Curves Ahead: Short Stories | *Wanted: One Groom*
Nobody's Perfect | *His Brother's Child* | *A Worthy Heir*
by Rebecca Brock—*The Giving Season*
& by Judy Bagshaw—*At Long Last, Love: A Collection*

NONFICTION:

Love is the Thread: A Knitting Friendship by Leslie Moïse, Ph.D.
Fat Poets Speak: Voices of the Fat Poets' Society—Frannie Zellman, Ed.
Ten Steps to Loving Your Body (No Matter What Size You Are) by Pat Ballard
Beyond Measure: A Memoir About Short Stature & Inner Growth by Ellen Frankel
Taking Up Space: How Eating Well & Exercising Regularly Changed My Life by Pattie Thomas, Ph.D. with Carl Wilkerson, M.B.A. (foreword by Paul Campos, author of *The Obesity Myth*)
Off Kilter: A Woman's Journey to Peace with Scoliosis, Her Mother & Her Polish Heritage—a memoir by Linda C. Wisniewski
Unconventional Means: The Dream Down Under—a spiritual travelogue by Anne Richardson Williams
Splendid Seniors: Great Lives, Great Deeds—inspirational biographies by Jack Adler

HEALING THE WORLD
ONE BOOK AT A TIME

CPSIA informa
Printed in the U
LVOW090736:

283415L

597 190619